BONSAI

BONSAI

Peter Chan

This edition published 2002 by
PRC Publishing Ltd,
64 Brewery Road, London N7 9NT
A member of the Chrysalis Group plc

Produced for Greenwich Editions
64 Brewery Road, London N7 9NT

ISBN 0 86288 427 6

Printed and bound in China

ACKNOWLEDGMENTS

Photographs have been credited by page number and position on the page. Abbreviations are as
follows: (t) top; (b) bottom; (l) left; (r) right, and combinations thereof. The publisher wishes to thank
Peter Chan for kindly supplying all the photography for this book, with the following exceptions:

Simon Clay for pages 2, 13, 19, 20, 22 (br), 23, 24 (tl, bl, br), 25, 27, 28, 29, 30, 34, 38 (and l back
cover), 40 (tl, bl), 41 (and tr back cover), 43, 44 (r), 47, 58 (all three), 61, 62, 63, 64, 67, 68, 70, 71, 72
(all), 73 (all), 74, 75, 84, 89, 90, 91 (all), 98, 104, 105, 106, 107, 108 (b), 109, 110, 111 (all),116 (all),
117, 118, 120 (all), 124, 125, 126 (all), 127 (all), 146, 151, 142,
143, 146, 150, 151

Marianne Marjeus for front cover, and pages 45, 52, 85, 131

Nasiruddin Yang for pages 12 & 14

Page 2: Japanese maple trained as a twin trunk bonsai.

Contents

BONSAI *Introduction*

The Far East and all its intriguing mysteries has held a fascination for Westerners from the very first days of contact. It is an interest compounded by the tales of adventure and risk brought back by early explorers and traders like Marco Polo. Eastern influences on the West include the different philosophies and religions of the Orient, which are often intimately linked with many intricate and skillful art forms. One of the most alluring of these is the art of bonsai—the growing of miniature trees and shrubs in a shallow confined container.

This book describes how to cultivate and maintain a bonsai for those new to the hobby, as well as those with a little more experience. Hints and tips are given for general care, along with

LEFT: In Japan, it is not uncommon to find traditional crafts, such as bonsai, living happily alongside high-tech industries. This is a nursery that specializes in the Japanese five needle pine.

RIGHT: Specimen pomegranate bonsai on the rooftop garden of a famous Japanese department store in the Ginza district of Tokyo. Good bonsai still fetch high prices in Japan.

ABOVE: A bonsai trained in the cascade style.

ABOVE: A bonsai of the famous Masahiko Kimura trained in the driftwood style.

more advanced techniques. Growing a bonsai is not difficult, but it does take a long time and is therefore ideal for the considered and spiritual gardener. When correctly cared for, a bonsai can be passed down as an heirloom from one generation to the next, becoming more prized and precious in the process, admired for its age and revered as a living reminder of those who have loved and cared for the plant over the decades.

Bonsai did not originate in Japan, as is often thought, although they have become intimately associated with Japanese culture and philosophy. Japanese display their favorite bonsai on important occasions at home in the *tokonoma*, an alcove designed for the display of artistic objects. At the New Year, for example, the *tokonoma* is traditionally filled with an apricot or plum tree in full blossom.

Old bonsai are magnificent plants, and if you are not fortunate enough to inherit one, they can be grown from ordinary seeds or cuttings, or for a quicker start, from nursery stock, including naturally stunted trees transplanted into containers. The financial value of an individual bonsai is an accumulation of its age, its species—some are more desirable or rarer than others, its aesthetic shape and size, and finally, whether it is cultivated or collected from the wild as a naturally occurring bonsai. Bonsai gleaned from the wild are the most valuable, as they are sculpted by nature, although this method of obtaining bonsai is not a recommended one. Naturally occurring

ABOVE: Bonsai of the famous Masahiko Kimura—widely acclaimed as the world's greatest bonsai master. His style has been copied by countless bonsai followers throughout the world.

bonsai are best left where they are. Favorite Japanese subjects to work with include varieties of juniper, pine, azalea, maple, and plum.

Bonsai is considered an art form, because it requires some skill to produce a beautiful, perfectly proportioned miniature tree that appears mature and to have survived the rigors of time and everything that the elements can throw at it. Each element of the tree is considered important, including the overall shape and the

angles of the branches, the quality and color of the leaves and bark, the shape and color of the trunk, and the structure of the roots. The crucial finishing touch is the container, as the wrong shape or color will detract from the harmony of the bonsai.

Bonsai are the progeny of ordinary trees or shrubs, not hybrid dwarf varieties, and a seed from a bonsai will grow into a normal full-sized tree if left untrained. Despite being smaller versions of

those left to grow naturally, bonsai can live at least as long as a normally grown plant of the same species. What they do need, however, is extra care with feeding and watering, due to their drastically reduced root run. Almost any tree or shrub can be used, regardless of the size it grows to in the wild, but for aesthetic reasons, species and varieties with small leaves make the best subjects, as they look more in proportion when the plant is mature.

Other characteristics to look for include varieties with small flowers, miniature fruit or berries, a plant that can produce a bark-like effect while still young, and finally, a tree that has a degree of pliability so that it can be trained into a pleasing shape. One word of warning: fruits cannot be miniaturized and need to be quickly removed if they show signs of becoming too big and heavy, so that they don't damage the delicate branches.

Although they are grown in containers, these miniature plants are primarily kept outdoors where they can enjoy the elements, as their larger siblings do. With the exception of some subtropical or tropical plants (a relatively recent innovation, specifically trained and grown for indoor culture), bonsai are not houseplants. If kept for too long inside, a bonsai will suffer, losing its leaves and dying quite quickly from the unaccustomed dry air and insufficient light. They can be brought inside for short periods of time, but they will not enjoy the experience and will need to resume their outside situation quickly.

There are many different styles of bonsai, which are grouped into three main categories: single trunk, multiple trunk, and multiple tree or group styles. Within these broad categories, such as the single trunk group, are classic styles, including formal upright, informal upright, slanting, semicascade, and cascade. A further refinement is the shape of the silhouette, of which there are six basics—round, pyramid, columnar, mushroom, broom (or besom), and inverted cone. Each of these shapes has a classic form that an afficionado can instantly recognize, and all are explained and illustrated in detail later in this book.

Within the second category—the multiple trunk group—bonsai have twin, triple, or multiple trunks, as well as the root connected or *netsunagari* style.

Sai Kei is an example of the third broad category—the multiple tree or group style. It is where two or more bonsai (Japanese favor an odd number of plants for aesthetic appeal) are gathered together in a landscape scene and often grouped around a rock feature. The intention here is to present the appearance of a coppice or grove of trees and extend the diverse range of artistic possibilities for bonsai.

A bonsai is kept small by careful branch and root pruning, occasional repotting into the same container, pinching off new growth, and careful wiring of the branches and trunk. In fact the size of a bonsai is immaterial; it can be any size for the subject and container, as long as there is an aesthetic appeal and sense of balance.

Most bonsai range in height from between 2 in. to 3 ft. The smallest bonsai, under 6 in. tall, are called *mame*, meaning "little bean," and are grown in pots the size of thimbles. At the other end of the scale are *man* trees, meaning "two, three, or more," a reference to the number of men needed to move it! However, most bonsai are between 1–2 ft. tall.

A bonsai tree is often positioned off-center in its container, not only because asymmetry is important to the visual effect, but the center point is symbolically where Heaven and Earth meet, and nothing else should occupy this significant place. Eastern philosophy is an integral part of bonsai. An important aesthetic principle is to create a visual sense of harmony by using a triangular composition. This expresses the relationship shared by the spirit (either a life-giving energy or deity), the artist, and the tree itself. Although it is a living thing, a bonsai is not dependent on the earth, as it is rooted within a container and is therefore a separate entity. It is complete in itself, yet still part of nature. This is what the Japanese mean by the expression "Heaven and Earth in one container."

RIGHT: The size of a bonsai is immaterial, as long as it has beauty and a sense of balance. With a small bonsai such as this one, it is possible to hold Heaven and Earth in the palm of your hand.

History of bonsai

The precise history of the cultivation of bonsai is far from clear. Evidence taken from ancient documents and manuscripts show or mention the growing of plants in containers in some of the very earliest gardens. The Hanging Gardens of Babylon, one of the Seven Wonders of the Ancient World, is thought to have had plants cultivated in pots.

There are several references to plants being kept in pots in Ancient Egypt; trees were planted into holes carved into the rock face and then into containers built for the purpose. At the same time, across the ocean in India, medicine men had started keeping jungle plants and herbs, which contained valuable medicinal properties necessary for their treatments and potions, in handy containers for convenient medicinal, as well as decorative, reasons. In fact, it is probable that bonsai first developed in India and then moved on to China. It is also known that the Romans kept trimmed plants in decorative pots.

By the second century, the contemplative Dyana Buddhists from India, practitioners of Ayurvedic medicine, used trimmed medicinal herbs growing in containers. They also discovered that some plants took on dwarfed characteristics after having their growth restricted for a few years. The monks took their horticultural knowledge with them into China where others with leisure time took up the practice. Inevitably, these were mostly Buddhist and Taoist monks, and certain high officials. These early practitioners of bonsai initially grew dwarfed trees that they found growing naturally in forests and on mountainsides. The more curved and ancient the plant, the more desirable it became and the more potent its spiritual powers were believed to be.

Although it is not difficult to grow plants in a container once you know how, these early gardeners had to acquire the knowledge needed for them to flourish. New horticultural techniques had to be developed to look after these special plants. No doubt many different types were tested, and there were many failures before reliable species were found. Chinese gardeners, rather than just growing plants in pots with no attempt at miniaturization, chose to cultivate individual trees or landscapes in a shallow bowl so that their root run was restricted and the plant intentionally became stunted. Their compositions were invariably quite large, and to complete the arrangement, they collected unusually shaped rocks and stones, which they incorporated into their small gardens of contemplation.

LEFT: Ficus religiosa, or the sacred Peepal tree, has been found here growing out of an ancient wall in central India. Material such as this is now collected and highly prized by bonsai enthusiasts in India.

The first clear reference to bonsai is in China, over a thousand years ago, in a tomb discovered from the Tang Dynasty (618–907). On the tomb of Prince Zhang Huai is a painting that shows bonsai-like trees being carried by servants. On one wall, a servant is seen carrying a miniature landscape, and on the other, a servant is carrying a pot containing a tree that clearly looks like a bonsai.

One ancient Chinese story speaks of the Han Dynasty (206 B.C.–A.D. 220) emperor who had his empire created in miniature across his palace courtyard. The garden contained rivers and lakes, trees, hills, and mountains in representation of his vast domain. This emperor loved to gaze over the landscape from the upper rooms of his palace and was so protective of his unique garden that no one else in the land was allowed so much as a miniature tree— on pain of death—for fear of evoking a threat to his empire.

In a practice known as *pun-sai*, the Chinese people grew single specimen trees in containers built for the

purpose; it is known to date back as far as the Heian era (eighth century), because of its inclusion in a picture in the biography of the priest Hounen-shoonin. The favored species were those that they believed to be invested with supernatural powers or actually contained spirits or gods, as well as plants that carried positive symbolism. These were frequently trained to look like animals, birds, serpents, and, especially, coiled dragons. Also, legendary characters were created, as well as cloud and smoke shapes. The tree trunks would be gnarled, and many of the leaves deliberately picked off to give a clearer view of the trunk. Also, the tree roots were partially exposed to show off their elaborate serpentine forms; the more tangled, the better. Sometimes miniature landscapes were assembled using small trees and rocks in a practice known as *Penjing*, or "tray scenery."

Buddhism had spread like wildfire across Asia through the work and

teachings of Zen Buddhist monks, taking with it the spirituality and contemplation so necessary to its practice. The growing of bonsai was an adjunct to their love of peace and quiet. Bonsai probably arrived in its spiritual homeland of Japan during the Heian period (794–1191). The exact date is uncertain, although it is possible that bonsai was cultivated by 1195, as there is a reference to it in a Japanese scroll of that period. There are few early written references to bonsai, but early art and painted scrolls show what can only be described as miniaturized plants growing in containers.

Buddhism had spread from India to Korea and then across the short stretch of water to the islands of Japan by the mid-sixth century. At this time, there was great exchange of culture and commerce between mainland China and Japan. Japanese envoys returned home to culture-hungry Japanese with many Chinese inventions, artifacts, behavior, and attitudes, and one of the most important influences, Buddhism. Suddenly, all things Chinese became the rage, including architecture, literature, music, ceremonies, the fine arts (especially calligraphy), and horticulture.

The Japanese already cultivated contemplative gardens called *shima* or "islands," a style still in favor today in Japan. Sometimes these would be replica models of specific locations showing the sea and islands; alternatively, they planted an imaginary landscape containing a pond with a central landscaped island complete with miniature trees. A variant of this was a dry scene consisting of carefully arranged sand and stones. Bonsai clearly appealed to the spiritual and artistic souls of Japanese gardeners, and they rapidly transformed the growing of miniaturized and trained plants to adapt to their unique culture and spirituality. They were excited by the possibilities of the latest Chinese horticultural ideas, but found them too elaborate. Instead, they reduced the design to *bonseki* or "tray rocks," just the bare essentials of a dry mountain landscape garden confined into a small box or tray.

Through Zen Buddhism, and to a lesser extent Taoism, bonsai came to represent a refined expression of humanity, nature, elements, and change. Tradition states that the three basic virtues known as *shin-zen-bi,* or truth, goodness, and beauty, are necessary to create a bonsai. Together these produce a channel for meditation and a bridge between humanity and nature.

However, the Japanese preferred a more refined view of such disciplined horticulture, and rather than create a whole landscape, they distilled their vision down to a single ideal tree. The Chinese may have invented bonsai, but the Japanese refined and formalized the art. The Japanese took to the art of bonsai with enthusiasm and extended it into undreamed-of realms. While the best specimens were still those gathered from the wild, many more small trees became available through mass propagation. Soon it wasn't just the Buddhist monks and their monasteries who owned bonsai, but also the aristocracy who demanded their own bonsai as a symbol of prestige and honor.

At first, in common with any rarefied foreign introduction, bonsai ownership was limited to the wealthy nobility, as well as monks and scholars who had the time and leisure for this new pastime. Bonsai does not seem to have spread to the lower classes for another 200 years or so until the fourteenth-century Muromachi era. Eventually everyone from a shogun down to merchants and even peasants could own a miniature tree. However, as with all fads, the fashion for bonsai faded somewhat as the *hachinoki,* trees in bowls, became so common that almost anyone could afford to own one. By now bonsai was viewed as a highly refined art form, implying that it must have been a well-established practice for many years. From then bonsai prospered, and by the sixteenth-century Edo era (1601–1867), bonsai were found in households across the land.

Most plants were still gathered from the wild as naturally stunted plants; the concept of pruning and training to create a miniaturized tree lay in the future. For the first time, a favorite bonsai would be brought into the Japanese home for a short period, for ceremonial or celebration purposes, and bonsai achieved the status of being a necessary ornament for important occasions.

The very few traders and missionaries allowed to enter seventeenth-century Japan from Western countries saw and described dwarf potted trees but dismissed them along with many

ABOVE: These antique bonsai pots are owned by a collector in Hong Kong. Many of the pieces date from the Tang dynasty.

other Eastern curiosities. Some traders even attempted to bring back such plants, but the specimens almost invariably died as Westerners had no understanding of the special care that they required (and perhaps were deliberately not told how to look after such specialized plants). This lack of understanding led to one of the most persistent misconceptions about bonsai: that they were only kept alive by mysterious and closely held secret Eastern practices.

In the seventeenth and eighteenth centuries, the Japanese cultural arts reached their peak, and consequently, such accomplishments were highly regarded in Japanese society. Bonsai was part of this cultural surge, and as gardeners increasingly understood horticultural requirements and especially of those for plants grown within the restriction of containers, they started to refine their pruning and training to grow ever more beautiful bonsai. Gardeners now concentrated on the removal of all but the most important parts of the plant until it was reduced to just the essential elements. Such ultimate refinement was very symbolic of the Japanese philosophy of this time; similarly, on a larger scale, Japanese gardens became stripped of all extraneous elements and were simplified to the

ABOVE: Specimen bonsai at the author's nursery in Surrey, England. They are mostly in the Japanese style and tradition.

bare bones. This reached its epitome with the garden around the Ryoan-ji temple.

Such intensive interest in horticulture encouraged some Japanese horticulturists to look back at traditional Chinese culture and philosophy, and in particular, they studied classical painting manuals. They decided that growing plants in pots was all well and good, but they wanted a purer, more Chinese interpretation of a single tree in a pot. This further refinement of growing a tree in a container they named "bonsai," a Japanese pronunciation of the Chinese word *pun-sai*. Bonsai were becoming better known and more widely grown in Japanese society, and shortly afterwards, a few Japanese manuals on the growing of such bonsai were published. All this greatly increased the demand for small trees collected from the wild and firmly established the art form within the culture of the country.

Bonsai now began to appear regularly in prints and illustrations of everyday Japanese life; even lowly merchants had their own plants, and competition for the best examples was fierce. The bonsai containers were enormously important and occasional competitions were held between potters for the best pots. By the eighteenth

century, bonsai had its own literature and forms, and this period is regarded as the peak of bonsai in both popularity and achievement.

Periodic Japanese bonsai magazines were appearing by the nineteenth century, and regular exhibitions were held. Special shallow pots were imported from China, and copper wire was beginning to be used for shaping branches and trunks. Different approaches to growing miniaturized trees evolved among bonsai growers. One extreme specialty concentrated on growing the smallest possible plants as *mame* ("bean") bonsai, the idea being to be able to hold the universe in the palm of your hand. This particular type of bonsai is still extremely popular today.

While bonsai was refined into a high art form in the East, the West remained largely ignorant of the culture until the mid-nineteenth century when Japan finally broke out of her self-imposed, 230-year isolation. Travelers were at last able to visit Japan, and they brought back descriptions of fantastic, seemingly aged, miniaturized trees contained in shallow ceramic pots. At last, in the late nineteenth century, bonsai were proudly brought to Europe and displayed for the first time to Western eyes. Bonsai were marveled at by thousands of eager visitors to the Paris Exhibitions of 1878, 1889, and 1900. In 1909, the London Exhibition brought the art form to an already educated horticultural public, and bonsai has never looked back. Its influence has emerged slowly, in keeping with such an ancient and contemplative tradition.

Interest, curiosity, and the desire to own such beautiful trees started to grow on gardeners, but others weren't so keen and thought the practice cruel. By 1900 in the United States, there were at least two Japanese nurseries selling bonsai, and a New York sale catalog dated 1904 shows that over 600 bonsai were auctioned in three days to an obviously eager public.

As technology improved, so did the tools for such a specialized skill. By the 1920s, Japanese horticulturists began to acquire specialized implements, including the concave-cutter. There was now a living to be earned in Japan from growing the plants. Two years after the Great Earthquake of 1923 devastated Tokyo, thirty local families of professional growers rebuilt their bonsai nurseries in a forest clearing on the northern edge of Omiya, a small town northeast of Tokyo. This assemblage of bonsai growers encouraged other interested parties to come to the village, and soon students were arriving to learn all about the refined art of bonsai. The village rapidly became the center of the bonsai world.

By the twentieth century, bonsai was firmly embedded in Japanese consciousness, and the first Kokufu Exhibition was held in Tokyo in 1934. The Kokufu Bonsai Ten exhibition, held annually in February at the Metropolitan Art Museum in Ueno Park, Tokyo, has become the most important annual bonsai show in the world. But, bonsai was developing all the time, and for such a slow discipline, it was remarkable in its evolution.

For example, in the mid-1930s, ideas about bonsai changed, and it became acceptable to interfere directly with the plant to create the shape of the tree rather than to rely on nature to sculpt the bonsai in an aesthetically pleasing manner. The beauty of the tree became paramount over any other spiritual or symbolic essence that it held. Fashions in bonsai began to be as important and changeable as fashions in art and culture. However, bonsai still represented a fusion of strong ancient beliefs with the Eastern philosophies of the harmony between humanity, the soul, and nature. During World War II, when Japan was at odds with the West, many Japanese even took their beloved bonsai with them to protect the plants from damage. After the war, interest in bonsai in the United States boomed; one persuasive theory points to the large number of GIs returning from service in Japan enthused with the hobby and passing it on to others. Also, the large Japanese-American population brought their hobby, as well as their knowledge and interest in bonsai, to a wider audience in America.

Interestingly, it was Japanese bonsai that took precedence in Europe and America, because the first teachers of the art form were from Japan. Furthermore, the Cultural Revolution in China forbade Chinese citizens from traveling out of their country and actively discouraged such personal luxuries. Therefore Japanese ideas have become the dominating view of bonsai, rather than Chinese.

ABOVE: A bonsai's pot is as important as the tree. Choose a pot that complements and creates an aesthetic sense of balance to the design.

It is only since the 1970s that the Chinese ideas of more wild-looking miniature landscapes has been brought to the West's attention. Chinese traditionally grow their plants on a bigger scale for display in courtyards and palace gardens. Chinese compositions of *penjing* can be as large as 10 ft. tall and 6 ft. or more wide.

In the twenty-first century, the demand for bonsai has never been greater. All around the world there are nurseries dedicated solely to bonsai growing, and many new species have been adapted to the art form. Plants suitable for different climates are grown, and difficult species are grafted onto reliable rootstock. The real pleasure comes from the satisfaction of creating your own plant, and this book will hopefully encourage more to try their hand at this wonderful hobby.

Chapter 1 – Types of Bonsai

Bonsai, although a fairly esoteric subject, has its classifications like any other pursuit. Every bonsai tree has its own distinctive features, yet it is possible to group them into convenient categories based on their common traits. Grouping bonsai in this way makes it easier to study and analyze the various aspects of each group and provides an easy reference for bonsai enthusiasts.

The Chinese were the first to devise a system of classification for this subject. It was based on the style of bonsai that was grown in each region, such as the Lingnan style of Southern China or the Suzhou style of the Shanghai area.

Over the years, bonsai practitioners have developed various systems of classification. Some are based on species, some on size but most importantly they are based on the shape of the tree. So bonsai have a straight trunk, some a slanting trunk; others are grow on rock or have driftwood incorporated into their design. The nar given to these different styles of bonsai convey an immediate ima, and provide a useful means of reference.

There has undoubtedly been an explosion of interest in bonsai over the past few years. There is hardly a country in the world to that does not have a group of bonsai enthusiasts. In countries as f away as Russia, Peru, India, or Sweden, the interest in bonsai is just intense. Bonsai enthusiasts are as fanatical about their hobby as an football or baseball fan. Bonsai books can be found in the most unlikely of places, as can the avid bonsai enthusiast, wiring and trimming away at his or her little tree. Bonsai enthusiasts in India c Bolivia are as well informed about the various styles and types of bonsai as the average Italian or American enthusiast. Terms such as "informal upright bonsai" or "cascade bonsai" have become, in a sense, an international language. This section aims to describe the various classifications.

LEFT: Adenium grown as a bonsai by an enthusiast in Jamshedpur, India. This plan is a succulent, rather than a tree, but it can be trained into a tree-like form.

RIGHT: This mountain maple, Acer palmatum matsumurae, was imported from Japan ten years ago by the author. It is 31½in. high.

There are many ways of classifying and describing bonsai, but there are essentially eight main groups that are discussed here: climate, whether they are evergreen or deciduous, species, size, where the source material comes from, if they are indoor or outdoor plants, and their country of origin. A knowledge of these categories will make bonsai growing easier and produce the best results.

ABOVE: A mango bonsai in Mumbai has full-sized fruit.

LEFT: This black pine began from seed over fourteen years ago and has a trunk diameter of 2¾ in. It has been grown in the ground and in pots.

CLIMATE

Bonsai are no longer the preserve of China, Korea, or Japan, but have spread to every corner of the world. And with the growth of the Internet, this interest is likely to increase even further.

Since a bonsai is a replica in miniature of a fully grown tree, the most suitable varieties for bonsai are those that are indigenous to the grower's own area. It is hardly surprising that the Japanese are fond of the Japanese maple for bonsai, and the people of Guangdong in Southern China, the tropical Elm, as these are the trees that will thrive in those areas. Bonsai that grow in the tropics are different from those that grow in temperate climates; those that flourish in Africa will not necessarily do well in northern Europe.

Classifying bonsai by the climate they are suitable for is a good starting point, as the care that they need and their growth habits will vary. Much of the success, or failure, of growing bonsai stems from understanding or not understanding the requirements of trees from different parts of the world. With the increase in the world trade of bonsai, this point becomes even more significant for those who are new to the hobby. It would be pointless to grow a Japanese maple in Calcutta or to grow a baobab in Scandinavia, because they both require very different conditions.

THIS PAGE: Chinese elm, 5 ft. high, Ching Chung Koon Taoist monastery, Hong Kong (top left); Shanghai-style bonsai, 4 ft. high (top right); 'Deshojo' maple, 37 in. high, author's collection (bottom).
RIGHT: Pinus sylvestris beuvronensis, 5 ft. high, author's collection.

ABOVE LEFT: The vibrant spring color of the maple 'Deshojo.'

ABOVE RIGHT: The new leaves of the South African fig Ficus 'Burt-Davyii.'

BELOW LEFT: The fruits of summer—a crab apple just turning color.

BELOW RIGHT: Gingko date from the Ice Age and were introduced from China into Japan in the eleventh century and to Europe in the mid-seventeenth century.

EVERGREEN OR DECIDUOUS

Tropical trees are for the most part evergreen, so this distinction is not as important for this type of climate. However, for those living in temperate regions, knowing whether a tree is evergreen or deciduous is especially useful.

In temperate areas, where winters are long, deciduous trees can be without their leaves for as long as six months, and this becomes a crucial factor when deciding which tree to grow. From a commercial point of view, for those running a plant center or nursery, knowing this information is important, too. Customers will want to know whether a tree is evergreen or deciduous to suit their particular preferences.

Most, but not all, evergreens in temperate regions are conifers, so it is worth checking that you have the right information about the plant that you choose to grow. For example, the larch and the ginkgo are conifers, but shed their leaves. There are many broad-leaved evergreens, too, such as eleagnus and members of the rhododendron family.

BOTANICAL SPECIES

Classifying bonsai by species is the most precise method of identification. Knowing the species and genera will tell you whether a tree is tropical or temperate and where their natural habitat is.

If you have a more accurate idea of a tree's growth habit, it is possible to train it into a style that best suits it. To train a tree into the cascade style, for example, it needs to have a fairly flexible stem. A tree that likes to grow strongly upright would not be suitable.

Knowing whether a tree is tropical or subtropical will indicate that it needs some form of protection during the winter and may possibly be suitable for keeping indoors. From knowing the botanical species, you will be able to precisely determine all these factors and provide growing conditions that achieve the best results.

RIGHT: This mountain maple is grown in the root-over-rock style. It measures 31½in. wide and 27½in. high. It has been in the author's collection for over fifteen years.

BELOW: The Satsuki azalea is one of the most popular flowering species used for bonsai. It is a lovely evergreen tree for most of the year, but in June it has the added bonus of producing a magnificent abundance of flowers.

LEFT: This massive five needle pine is not strictly a bonsai, as it is meant to be a Japanese garden tree. It is nevertheless trained in exactly the same way.

SIZE

To the average person not familiar with the subject, a bonsai is a tree no more than a foot high, but in fact, bonsai come in many sizes. Major exhibition trees in Japan can be 30 in. high, while those in China can be as much as 12 ft. or even 15 ft. tall. As can be seen from this example, there are no hard and fast rules about size.

With such variations in physical size, a system of classification has been devised for this criterion alone, broadly based on the Japanese system. Very tiny bonsai, or *mame* (pronounced mah-may), are usually less than 2–3 in. high; small bonsai, or *shohin*, are usually 6–7 in. high; medium bonsai are 12–20 in. high; and large bonsai are 2–4 ft. high. In China, it is not unusual to see extra-large bonsai that are 20 ft. high in ceramic or marble pots 15–20 ft. long.

However, this classification by size is only an arbitrary system, devised mainly for competition purposes. Otherwise, it is a purely personal preference. There are some who prefer the magnificence of larger bonsai, and others who like the daintiness of smaller trees.

For those living in apartments with only a balcony, smaller bonsai are usually the only sensible option. Those who are fortunate to own a decent size garden will be able to keep much larger bonsai.

For the real enthusiast, such obstacles are not a problem. In Hong Kong where most people live in tiny apartments, large bonsai are grown in the bonsai club's garden many miles away from the city center. Size preference is a personal choice and not determined by strict guidelines; each has its place in the vast panoply of bonsai styles.

RIGHT: A cotoneaster is grown in the root-over-rock style. It is only 5 in. high and is classed as a shohin bonsai.

SOURCE MATERIAL

A bonsai can be created from a number of sources. You could create a bonsai from a tree growing in your own garden, from part of a hedge, or from a plant found growing in a mountain or forest in the wild. Depending on the source of the tree, the training regime or program will vary quite considerably.

There was a time when it was commonly thought that all bonsai had to be grown from seeds and cuttings. This gave rise to the notion that making a good bonsai could take years and was seldom achievable in one's lifetime. Fortunately, this is not true. There are many different ways of creating bonsai—some are less consuming than others.

Seeds and cuttings are a viable source of commercial bonsai, provided they are allowed a period of rapid growth in the open ground. In open ground the trunks thicken rapidly, thereby giving the look of age in a relatively short space of time. Alternatively, nursery material, which has already been grown for a number of years, could be used as a source for mature bonsai. Increasingly now, bonsai nurseries are cultivating their own raw material for enthusiasts to use as stock plants. Junipers, pines, larches, and maples are favorite subjects for this type of work.

Material collected from the wild has always been the most prized source of bonsai raw material. However, the increasing awareness of the need to protect the environment has made people think twice about using this source for making bonsai. Sadly, there are numerous collectors who take material from the wild, but bonsai enthusiasts should exercise greater responsibility and restraint in this matter.

LEFT: Cedars and spruces can be purchased from nurseries by enthusiasts for making into bonsai.

RIGHT: This magnificent five needle pine at a Japanese bonsai nursery was created from material collected from the wild, or yamadori ("collected from the mountains"). Material collected from the wild has always been the most prized source of bonsai raw material, but an increased awareness of the need to protect the environment has made it less of a viable option.

INDOOR OR OUTDOOR BONSAI

Indoor bonsai are like houseplants, mainly tropical and subtropical trees that are sold in Europe and North America for the indoor plant market. It could be argued that there is no such thing as an indoor bonsai because in their native habitat, bonsai would grow outdoors in warm tropical conditions and bright sunshine.

In an indoor environment, they can never perform as well because the average living room cannot replicate their natural environment. Those without a garden or patio to grow plants may still want to keep bonsai, however, and need trees that can be kept in a reasonable condition inside the house. Despite the difficulties of keeping them indoors, they are still fun to grow, and anyone blessed with a green thumb will most likely be successful.

Traditional outdoor bonsai are less troublesome. Provided they are watered regularly when necessary, usually in the spring and summer, they can live for many years.

ABOVE: Star fruit on a bonsai in a suburban Mumbai garden. They flourish in the hot, sunny, and humid conditions of the tropics. In a living room in the northern hemisphere, the tree would almost certainly die.

RIGHT: Tropical bonsai are best grown as outdoor plants, which is how they are grown in India. It would be difficult to grow plants like these indoors in the West, as they quickly deteriorate.

COUNTRY OF ORIGIN

With the increasing popularity of bonsai, there isn't a country in the world where bonsai is not grown. The choice of variety is usually indigenous to the country they are being grown in, and the styles and shapes are now beginning to reflect the cultural and aesthetic preferences of different nations.

Different cultures will find certain ways of presenting a style more aesthetically pleasing than others, which leads to differences in the styles from each country. Although China, Japan, and Korea have made important contributions to the development of this art, other cultures are beginning to present their own particular style of bonsai. Japanese bonsai is as different from Chinese bonsai as Italian is from American. One country's preference is not superior or inferior to another, but a true bonsai lover will recognize a good bonsai from a bad one, no matter where it is from.

It is only to be expected that bonsai differ in style from country to country. However, climate is by far the most significant factor. In countries such as the United States, which has a wide variation in climate, bonsai growers will be all too familiar with the problems of growing plants in an area unsuited to it. Plants that grow well in tropical Florida, for example, will not grow well in upstate New York. The same can be said of other large countries, such as Australia, Russia, and India. Climate is one of the most critical factors in determining what can be grown in a particular area. Stick to what grows best in your area, and work at perfecting the shapes and styles suited to those species.

LEFT: Chinese elm in the informal upright style. This bonsai is typical of the tropical bonsai produced in southern China for the indoor European and North American market. Elms grow rapidly in tropical conditions and are therefore easy to train. They are cost-effective to produce and consequently economic to buy. This variety is one of the easiest subjects for growing as indoor bonsai, because they tolerate a wide temperature range.

RIGHT: Triple trunk 'Dehojo' maple imported from Japan. This very elegant tree is 3 ft. in height. Maples are cool temperate trees and cannot be grown in the tropics. Even in the milder Mediterranean regions, they struggle to survive.

35

SHAPE AND STYLE

For most bonsai practitioners, the formally recognized styles used by the Chinese and Japanese provide the main guidelines for classification. The style or shape of bonsai can be grouped into three main generic classes based on the number of trunks used in the design.

These are:

(a) The single trunk styles: The variegated uzen elm (below) is a good example of the informal upright style, which is the most widely used single trunk style in bonsai.

(b) The multiple trunk styles: Trunks in this style usually emerge from one central point forming a cluster of stems. The five needle pine (opposite) from a bonsai nursery in western Saitama, Japan, was collected from the wild many years ago. It is huge in bonsai terms, measuring 4 ft. high and 5 ft. wide.

C

(c) The multiple tree or group styles: This is often referred to as the "forest style." The Japanese have often insisted on using an odd number of trees for their group plantings, largely for aesthetic reasons.

This can sometimes be taken too far when the number of trees in the group exceeds nine. When there are too many trees, the eye cannot assimilate, let alone differentiate between odd and even numbers, so this rule seems a little pedantic.

This group of Japanese larch (left) was created from ordinary nursery material and forms part of the author's collection. The contrast in height makes it very distinctive. The tallest tree is 4 ft. high.

Within these broad categories are subgroups. In the single trunk category, there are the following styles:

(a) Formal upright or *chokkan* style: A Hinoki cypress (below) imported from Japan some years ago shows the desired tiered formation of the branches, which have to be trimmed constantly to keep them in shape. The trunk is perfectly straight.

(b) Informal upright or *moyogi* style: This Chinese Juniper (below) is a good example of the informal upright style, sometimes referred to as the "S shape" or "pine style." It is the popular image of the bonsai.

C

(c) Slanting, or *shakkan*, style: The combination of the driftwood and the slanting style works well for the Chinese juniper (left). The driftwood makes the tree look genuinely old, while the slant gives the impression of immense tenacity against the forces of nature.

(d) Broom, or *hokidachi*, style: The broom style is invariably used with deciduous trees. Species such as Japanese gray bark elm, *Zelkova serrata*, (shown below left) and kiyo-hime maple are favorite subjects for this style. They look their best in winter without their leaves. The bonsai shown here has just had its leaves pruned to give more light to the delicate branches.

(e) Cascade, or *kengai*, style: This is a classic style derived from ancient Chinese tradition. This Chinese juniper (opposite), imported from Japan, is 3 ft. in length.

(f) Literati, or *bunjin*, style: This is another classic Chinese style bonsai. The Japanese five needle pine (below) was imported from Kyushu, Japan, in 1990.

d

f

e

(g) Windswept, or *fukinagashi,* style: This is a very natural style that simulates trees battered by the elements. It is common to find trees like this growing along the coast. This larch (right), 27 in. high, was collected over twenty-five years ago. The top had died, so it was made into driftwood. With just one branch left alive, the windswept style was the natural choice.

(h) Driftwood, or *sharimiki,* style: Carving driftwood effects on bonsai must be done sympathetically and be appropriate for the style and context of the tree. Look at the many trees in nature that have dramatic and elegant driftwood, and use them as inspiration. This needle juniper, *Juniper rigida,* (below) is reputed to be 300–500 years old. The trunk has a 12 in. diameter and is eighty percent dead driftwood, but is perfectly healthy.

(i) Split trunk, or *sabamiki*, style: This Chinese juniper, 4 ft. high, has driftwood to emphasize the style.

(j) Semicascade, or *han kengai*, style (not shown).

(k) Weeping, or *shidare* style (not shown).

(l) Root-over-rock, or *seki joju*, style: The colorful berries of this pyracantha is an added bonus in the fall.

(m) Planted on rock, or *ishi seki*, style: Collected thirty years ago, this larch was planted on limestone and is now 27½ × 27½ in.

(n) Exposed root, or *neagari*, style (not shown).

Within the multiple trunk category there are the following styles:

(a) Twin trunk, or *sokan,* style (not shown).

(b) Triple trunk, or *sankan,* style:

The '*Deshojo*' maple (right), 43 in. high, was imported more than twelve years ago from Japan.

(c) Multiple trunk, or *kabudachi,* style:

Trunks emerging from a central point (shown below) are trained to create a sense of balance.

(d) Root connected, or *netsunagari,* style:

The root connected style simulates what often happens in nature when an old tree is uprooted in a storm. When a tree falls on its side, it can still survive by putting out new branches that eventually grow into individual trees. This grove of needle juniper (far right) is the *yatsu-busa* type of *Juniperus rigida*. It is 35 in. high and grows from one central stem.

Finally, within the multiple tree or group category, there are the following styles:

(a) Group planting, or forest known as *yose ue*: The forest style is appealing because it looks completely natural. It looks so realistic, it only requires miniature birds to fly through it to complete the scene. This Japanese mountain maple forest (below), shown in the fall, has thirty-five trees, the tallest of which is 41 in. high.

(b) Group planted on rock: This trident maple root over rock (right) is unusual, because it is made up of several trees planted over a flat piece of red Japanese waterworn stone. Most trident maple root over rock compositions are made to resemble single trees, but this is quite different.

(c) Landscape, or *sai kei* (not shown).

a

THE INFORMAL UPRIGHT STYLE

The informal upright style is perhaps the most commonly encountered style in bonsai. It encompasses any style that does not fall strictly within the definition of the other more formal styles. For example, trees with a bent trunk or those that fork high up from the base, in fact anything out of the ordinary, can be grouped under this category. Generally speaking, bonsai that have S-shaped trunks are in the informal upright style. Some bonsai practitioners refer to this style as the "pine style," because it is similar to the way five needle pines grow. Although bonsai in this style are often found growing naturally like this, the shape can be achieved quite easily by wiring.

The style requires a tapered trunk, like the formal upright, but is closer to the way a tree would naturally look when exposed to the elements from an early age. Branches are positioned to give the trunk a sense of balance and should ideally grow from the outside of the curves and not on the inside. The crown of the tree is usually full and directly above the base of the tree. *Jin*, the carving of dead branches to look like dead limbs of a tree, is more appropriate and effective for the informal upright style.

Many species of plants are suitable for this design, including the Chinese juniper, maple, beech, practically all conifers, and some ornamental trees, such as crab apple, cotoneaster, and pomegranate.

LEFT: This five needle pine is a rugged old tree and typical of the informal upright or myogi style. Pines like this are still produced by the thousand in central and southern Japan.

RIGHT: In nature, trees bend away from the wind or shade towards the light. An informal upright bonsai should be trained to bend to the left or right and not toward the viewer. The branches on this bonsai are arranged to balance the composition in proportion to the size and the shape of the trunk.

RIGHT: A Japanese Honeysuckle, Lonicera morrowii, *in the informal upright style, shows the conical shape that is typical of bonsai. The trunk, 5 in. in diameter, is quite thick and the twists and bends in it give it an interesting appearance. It flowers profusely throughout the summer.*

LEFT: The S-shaped trunk of this Chinese juniper bonsai, in the informal upright style, is what is normally considered a bonsai. Little bits of driftwood called jins *and* sharis, *or weathered deadwood, emphasize the powerful-looking trunk. This particular bonsai has flowing lines and a graceful appearance. Junipers are easy to keep and therefore very suitable for beginners. They are extremely hardy and are very resistant to drought, strong sunshine, and low temperatures. It is an evergreen and will provide interest all year round.*

THE CASCADE STYLE

The cascade is probably one of the most sophisticated styles in the art of bonsai. It is a timeless design, which has its origins in the brush stroke paintings of the ancient Chinese literati scholars, dating back to around A.D. 500 or 600. These brilliant artists were inspired by the pines they saw growing from cliffs in the mountains that were surviving under the harshest of conditions. These trees were not just visually inspiring, but gave spiritual and philosophical insight to the artists that painted them.

The sight of such beautiful trees surviving against the harsh elements represented to them the survival of the human spirit. The trees' tenacity also symbolized the existence of beauty in the midst of extreme adversity. Capturing both the spirit and beauty of these rugged trees in their paintings, these Chinese artists in turn provided a source of inspiration for later generations of bonsai artists.

For the past few centuries, Chinese, Korean, and Japanese bonsai growers have continued using the cascade style simply because it is a beautiful and elegant design. Drawing inspiration from art and nature, growers have continued with the cascade style through the centuries until today, where among contemporary bonsai enthusiasts, it is established as a firm favorite.

If done properly, this style gives the impression of a tree bent by the forces of gravity, as it would appear in nature. The trunk usually twists as if to emulate a meandering stream, and the branches provide a sense of graceful balance to the composition.

To a bonsai lover, seeing trees cascading from cliff faces and mountain crags is a sheer joy. These dramatic sights can be found all over the world, in the Himalayas, the Alps, the Rockies, and even in the moutains of Wales and Scotland.

Design characteristics

The cascade style of bonsai is unique in horticulture, because the tree grows downward rather than upward. This is something that is at complete odds with nature, because all trees and plants grow upward toward the light in normal conditions. However, cascade trees grow in abnormal circumstances, and the cascade style of bonsai is an attempt to mimic this anomaly. When a tree grows out of a rock crevice, the weight of its trunk eventually pulls it down, forcing it to lean over and grow in the form of a cascade. Parts of the tree will try to grow upward, usually in the form of a small apex, but the overall direction is downward.

The typical design of a cascade bonsai, which copies this unusual form of growth as it appears in nature, is a long branch or main trunk that hangs downward with a small head or apex growing at the top. Sometimes a cascade may not have a head or apex at all, but just a long arm or cascading branch. This can look equally effective, as the trunk is exposed and can be fully appreciated.

If the trunk or main branch hangs down below the foot of the pot, it is referred to as a "full cascade." If, on the other hand, the main branch ends somewhere midway between the rim and the base of the pot, then it is referred to as the "semicascade style." Many species are suitable if they have flexible trunks and are not strongly upright.

RIGHT: This bonsai was made from nursery stock material about fifteen years ago. It is a Scots pine with very small needles and is nearly 3 ft. in height.

Suitable species for the cascade style

As with most bonsai, you can use any variety of tree to make a cascade as long as it is pliable enough to take the desired shape. Young Scots pine, larch, cotoneaster, beech, ash, 'Blaauw' juniper, *Juniperus squamata*, oak, and even maple are all suitable subjects for cascades. However, the preferred species used for most of the classic cascade bonsai in China and Japan are evergreens such as white or black pine, yew, Chinese juniper, podocarpus, and ezo spruce.

This does not mean that deciduous varieties cannot be used. A magnificent specimen of a Japanese mountain maple is now one of the show trees at Herons Bonsai, as well as a very gnarled, old Japanese hornbeam, in the semicascade style, which came from Japan in the mid-sixties. Satsuki azaleas are used as cascades occasionally.

In the mountainous regions of Europe, mugo and Scots pine, many varieties of spruces, common juniper, yew, ash, and hawthorn grow naturally in the cascade style. Many of these specimens are invariably old trees and should be respected. Venerable, wild trees are better left as they are to be simply admired in their natural habitat. Even if the magnificent old junipers growing out of high limestone cliffs overlooking the sea look wonderfully tempting to collect, taking trees from such a beautiful spot would not be advised.

Nursery stock

Nursery stock is a renewable resource and since many varieties have a habit of growing along the ground, it is an excellent source for material. Many of the prostrate junipers are suitable for the cascade style for this reason. *Juniperus procumbens*, *Juniperus horizontalis*, *Juniperus chinensis* 'San Jose,' *Juniperus communis* 'Green Carpet,' and *Juniperus communis* 'Hornibrookii' are all excellent subjects for cascade. Well-established nursery plants will invariably have many branches. The secret is to select the best one for the main trunk line. Don't be afraid to reduce the number of branches on a nursery plant. Very often, as much as seventy percent of the plant will have to be removed in order to reveal the main trunk line.

The main criterion in deciding what to keep and what to remove is to find a trunk that has an interesting zigzag shape. Once you have established this, try and find a secondary branch, which will serve as the head. This will usually be a thinner branch, which can be wired back on itself to form the apex or head. The secondary branches along the trunk line are easy to select. Simply choose branches that are evenly spaced along the trunk and emanate from the elbows, or outer edge of a curve, and not from inside. Remove all unnecessary branches from above and below the trunk line.

LEFT: This Japanese mountain maple is rather unusual, as maples are seldom trained in the cascade style. It has been shown at the Chelsea Flower Show, England. In the fall, the leaves turn a magnificent flame red.

RIGHT: This is a Chinese juniper trained in the classic cascade style complete with crown and cascading tiers of branches.

Bending techniques

It is best to use a plant that already has a cascade or semicascade trunk, as anything over ½ in. in diameter will be extremely difficult to bend. It is possible to bend thick trunks by a combination of splitting branches and wiring. Using the Japanese branch splitting tool, sometimes known as the "trunk cracker" in Japanese books, the trunk can be split into two or more segments to make bending easier. By splitting the trunk into laminated sections, the wood becomes more pliable and, like plywood, is much easier to bend. Wrapping the trunk in raffia before bending it also helps, as it protects the branch from splitting when excessive pressure is applied.

When bending the main trunk, try and introduce cascading steps into the design, and while making a zigzag in the trunk, keep the secondary branches in mind. Ideally they should emerge from the outer edge, or elbows, of the bends.

ABOVE: The growing tip of a cascade bonsai reaches to the base of its container. A cascade pot needs to be tall to complement and incorporate this design. Evergreen bonsai trained in this style usually have a rectangular, brown, unglazed pot as shown here.

Pots suitable for cascades

Cascade pots are tall so that the main cascading branch can hang downward freely. They are usually square in shape, although hexagonal, round, and octagonal tops are also acceptable. Glazed pots are used for deciduous trees, while unglazed brown, rust, and gray tones are best for evergreen conifers.

Tall pots drain well, but using a free-draining potting soil is still important whatever the species.

Tips for the care of cascade trees

The cascade is not the easiest style to grow for a number of reasons. It is a cumbersome tree and the main cascading branch can get damaged easily. When transporting a cascade bonsai, lie it on its side or strap it to a milk crate or box so that the cascading branch is uppermost to protect it from knocks and accidents.

When displaying a cascade bonsai on a bench at home, make sure the tree is securely fastened down to keep it from toppling over in strong winds or being knocked over by children or pets.

Perhaps the most difficult aspect of care is maintaining vigor at the tip of the plant. Because the sap on all trees flows upward, getting the sap to flow downward, as it needs to in this style, can be quite a problem. Some people try to overcome this problem by placing the tree on its side. This can work, but the secret probably lies in keeping the tree very healthy so that the nutrients reach every part, including the furthest tip.

There are many ways of achieving or making a good-looking cascade bonsai. Once you have the horticultural skills, achieving a good design comes with practice. Look at examples of cascade trees in books, magazines, and bonsai nurseries that import quality trees from Japan and China and don't be afraid to copy. Ingenuity and imagination will take you forward, just as the makers of the original cascade trees were inspired by the paintings and high ideals of the Chinese literati scholars. Part of the enjoyment of bonsai is the pursuit of excellence, but your own enjoyment comes from simply doing it. Excellence will soon follow.

THE LITERATI STYLE

Of all the styles in bonsai, the literati style is probably the most sophisticated. It is a beautiful style, both elegant and lovely, yet deceptively simple. It is not to everyone's liking, however, and is generally an acquired taste. To appreciate it fully requires a certain degree of understanding that only comes from education and an appreciation of Chinese art.

It is a style reminiscent of ancient pines, which tend to shed their lower branches as they get old. The focal point of the design is the trunk, which needs to be full of character. The branches are limited to the uppermost part of the trunk and should bear just enough foliage to keep the tree healthy and vigorous.

Originally a Chinese style, literati has its origins in the intelligentsia of ancient China. The great scholars of the Tang dynasty (or possibly earlier dynasties) devoted a great deal of their energies to painting, poetry, and perhaps even bonsai. The paintings of the pine trees that they saw in the mountains and the miniatures that they themselves cultivated had a certain artistic flair, which only these learned men were able to create.

With just a stroke of the brush, they could capture the essence of a lonely pine on the mountainside in all its stark beauty. These hauntingly beautiful images were largely of sinuous trees with tall, slender trunks. Over the centuries, the Japanese grew to appreciate this particular form of art, which they unashamedly copied from China.

The Japanese scholars who pursued this form of art were called *bunjin,* or literary men. Like the Chinese scholars before them, they were the cream of society, and high art was their exclusive province. No one else had the capacity to appreciate the artistic pursuits that these men dabbled in. Over a period of time, the bonsai that these literary men admired and created came to be referred to as "*bunjin* type bonsai."

RIGHT: Japanese five needle pine trained in the literati, or bunjin, *style. This tree has its own roots and has not been grafted.*

Chapter 2 – Success with Bonsai
Hints and Tips

CHOOSING AND BUYING BONSAI

An expertly trained bonsai is a work of art, but it is not, as many would imagine, a special type or species of plant. A bonsai is a tree or shrub grown in a container and shaped to resemble a miniaturized version of a fully grown tree as it appears in nature. The aim is to keep the tree small and beautiful by the skillful manipulation and pruning of the trunk and branches to slow its growth. Any tree or shrub can be turned into a bonsai—junipers, beech, maple, pine, and even trees with large leaves, such as horse chestnut, make beautiful miniature trees.

BELOW: A selection of indoor bonsai on display in a nursery. These are mainly warm temperate trees suitable for cool, indoor conditions.

Indoor and outdoor bonsai

Most European and American bonsai dealers will offer two main types of bonsai that can be grown indoors or outdoors. Indoor bonsai are like houseplants, which are mainly tropical and subtropical species suitable for keeping indoors. They are slightly more difficult to keep than the outdoor varieties. Bonsai purists would argue that there is no such thing as indoor bonsai, because they are in fact tropical trees that grow outdoors in their native habitat. An average living room cannot replicate tropical conditions, and consequently they seldom do well. However, they are still fun to grow and if you have a green thumb, there is no reason why you should not be successful.

Traditional outdoor bonsai are less troublesome. Provided they are watered regularly in the summer and periodically in winter, they can live for many years.

BELOW: A selection of hardy outdoor bonsai.

Which varieties are best?

Most of the indoor bonsai sold in the West come from southern China, and some of the best varieties include serissa, sageretia, ficus, pomegranate, Chinese elm, carmona, jasmine orange, ligustrum, podocarpus, eugenia, and nandina.

Some are easier to keep than others. Chinese elm, ficus, and pomegranate take to indoor conditions quite well. The others require much more care and attention, especially with regard to light, humidity, and temperature levels. Most hardy outdoor varieties are relatively trouble free. White pine, Chinese juniper, beech, zelkova, and maples are some of the more popular outdoor species.

Where to buy

A specialty bonsai nursery is the best place to get sound advice and a good selection of trees, pots, and accessories. Some garden centers stock bonsai, and provided the staff is knowledgeable and the bonsai look healthy, you can buy from them with confidence.

Avoid buying outdoor bonsai that have been kept for a prolonged period in unsuitable indoor conditions, such as in stores that are poorly lit and much too warm. If they have been kept in these conditions for any length of time, the chances are that they will have deteriorated and will be more prone to pests and diseases.

How much should a bonsai cost?

Prices will vary from country to country, and depend very much on the beauty of the tree, the species, and age. Indoor bonsai are slightly cheaper because they are mostly imported from tropical countries where they grow much faster and trees are generally cheaper.

Outdoor varieties, which are imported mainly from Japan, tend to be slightly more expensive. Good quality bonsai are like fine antiques. Some reach the status of collectors' items, and large specimens of exhibition trees can command very high prices. Desirable bonsai in Japan, like fine paintings, frequently change hands for several million yen, or over eight thousand dollars.

Choosing the best one

A good bonsai should look healthy. If it is an evergreen, the foliage should be fresh and green. A deciduous tree should have tight, healthy, twiggy growth with no dead branches or shriveled up leaves.

If a bonsai is healthy and well established, nursery staff should have no qualms about showing you the state of the rootball, unless it has just been repotted.

Check that the tree is firm in its pot and check that the soil is loose and porous, moist but not waterlogged. The pot must have adequate drainage holes, which are not blocked. Make sure there are no wire marks on the trunk and that it has a natural shape and taper.

ABOVE: This pine has a healthy rootball. The white film over the roots is a beneficial fungus—mycorrhiza normally found on pines. A compact root system is a good indication of a well grown and healthy plant.

RIGHT: Evergreen bonsai on display in the classic Japanese style. Ideally, bonsai should be displayed at eye level.

GENERAL CARE AND ROUTINE MAINTENANCE

It is no good buying a very beautiful tree if you cannot keep it alive. Watering is by far the single most important task in ensuring that the tree does not die. Because bonsai are grown in pots, they need to be watered at least once a day in dry weather or more frequently if it is very warm and dry. Even in winter, if it has not rained for some time, bonsai need to be watered.

The right kind of soil, where the bonsai is positioned, and how often it is fed are other crucial factors to ensure the success of caring for a bonsai. How to repot your bonsai and trimming the roots and shoots are also discussed in this section.

Watering

Outdoor bonsai are much easier to care for than indoor bonsai. Outdoor bonsai can be left in the open all year except in very frosty conditions. Daily watering from spring to autumn is essential, and on very hot days, watering twice a day may be necessary. During winter, outdoor bonsai generally do not need watering, as the rain and dampness is usually sufficient to keep the tree alive. Be sure to check the soil from time to time to ensure that it is damp. If there has been no rain for a prolonged period of time, then you may need to water.

Protecting the trees in an unheated greenhouse during winter is a good idea, but they will need to be checked regularly to make sure they are not dry. If they are dry, then they will need watering. During winter it is best to water them in midmorning, provided the temperature is not below freezing. On sunny days in winter, trees that are kept in the greenhouse should be brought out for an airing. Alternatively, make sure the greenhouse is well ventilated to reduce the risk of fungal disease.

Indoor bonsai need watering all year round as they dry out much more quickly inside the house. The soil should be damp at all times, but not soaking wet. Never let the soil dry out completely. Should this ever happen, all the leaves will shrivel. If this happens, you can still revive the tree by removing all the dead leaves. Bonsai in small pots will need to be watered more frequently than those in larger pots, as small pots dry out more quickly. A daily check is therefore essential. If you stand your indoor bonsai on a shallow tray of sand or gravel, this will help to maintain humidity around the tree.

RIGHT: Watering should never be a chore. It can be a very relaxing exercise at the end of a busy day. It is said that it takes a lifetime to perfect the art of watering bonsai. This is certainly true, as it takes quite a lot of experience to judge how much and how frequently a bonsai should be watered.

What makes a good bonsai soil?

Every bonsai enthusiast will have his or her own favorite soil recipe, but there is no such thing as a universal or ideal bonsai potting soil, because different species have different soil needs. Most growers usually have different mixes for different bonsai, modified to suit the type and age of tree.

A basic understanding of what plants need in order to grow is a good starting point in any discussion on soil. All plants need moisture, air, and nutrients for healthy root development, and the soil is the single most important medium through which these needs are met. An ideal soil must have the capacity to drain freely, but at the same time be able to hold moisture to sustain the tree. It must also be able to allow air to flow through the soil particles so that the roots can breathe. Last but not least, the soil must be able to retain sufficient nutrients to feed the tree. How these different properties are combined together will determine the suitability of a potting soil for a particular type of bonsai.

Loam-based potting soil used by cacti and succulent growers, with some modification, can meet the needs of most bonsai. By adding varying amounts of sharp sand or other drainage material, the soil structure can be considerably enhanced.

For instance, pines and junipers thrive in a potting soil that is predominantly sand. You could add as much as fifty percent coarse grit or sand to a cacti potting soil to use for pine and juniper bonsai. For broad-leaved varieties, such as maples, hornbeam, and beech, add a third more fine bark or peat. For fruiting and flowering trees, add a little more peat and well-rotted horse manure to the general mix. If you prefer mixing your own potting soil, then try using one part sphagnum moss peat, two parts fine bark, two parts coarse sand, and one part Japanese *akadama* for general use.

LEFT: A good bonsai compost is one that drains freely. You can't go wrong by adding lots of gritty material.

RIGHT: This root over rock trident maple is planted in pure akadama—*the Japanese red clay soil. Maples thrive in this type of soil.*

The Japanese use a special growing medium called *akadama* made from red clay granules. This is suitable for most bonsai and has the unique property of being able to drain and hold moisture at the same time. It is widely used in Japan and can be purchased from some bonsai nurseries. Peat-based potting soil can be used for indoor bonsai and small seedlings. It is not very suitable for larger trees, as it can dry out very rapidly and does not have the body to physically support the tree in its pot. Many indoor bonsai from China are planted in river clay. This is fine for bonsai growing in humid tropical conditions, but is difficult to manage in average living room conditions. Indoor bonsai will fare a lot better if planted in a peat-based potting soil with additional sand added.

Position

Most bonsai prefer a bright, sunny position, sheltered from strong winds and drafts. Trees in small pots may fare better if kept in partial shade, as they could dry out very quickly on hot, sunny days. Trees grown in full sun are healthier, as long as the leaves do not scorch. Exposure to the sun also induces better autumn coloring on deciduous trees and helps to promote flower buds on fruiting and flowering species. In winter, most outdoor bonsai would benefit from some protection, and many enthusiasts keep their trees either in an unheated greenhouse or under bonsai staging.

Indoor bonsai are best kept on a bright windowsill and away from drafts. They should never be placed in a dark corner of a room, as this will cause them to shed their leaves and weaken. Indoor bonsai will benefit from some time outdoors during the summer. They can be kept outdoors as soon as the temperature rises above 65°F, from around June to mid-September.

RIGHT: Always grow bonsai in good light—something all plants need for healthy growth. It also helps to ripen the sugars in the leaves, which in turn produces the glorious, rich fall colors in deciduous trees.

Feeding

All bonsai should be fed with a fertilizer at regular intervals—usually once a month in order to keep them healthy and vigorous. Contrary to popular belief, bonsai are not starved in order to keep them dwarfed. Feeding should only be done during the growing season, which, in the case of outdoor trees in the temperate region, is from April to September.

For indoor trees, feeding should be done throughout the year, but less frequently during the winter. Outdoor bonsai benefit from a high nitrogen feed in the spring, but later in the summer, a low nitrogen fertilizer should be used. Use either liquid feed or fertilizer pellets.

BELOW: Feeding is absolutely essential for bonsai, as the pots are small, and the availability of nutrients is somewhat restricted. Pellet and liquid fertilizers are good. As a rule, young trees need more feeding than older ones.

Repotting or trimming the roots

One of the common misconceptions about bonsai is that the roots are trimmed regularly to dwarf the tree. Many newcomers to the hobby take this quite literally and kill their bonsai by doing this too frequently. The root trimming process, or repotting, should only be carried out when a tree becomes pot-bound. The frequency of repotting depends on the vigor of the bonsai. Some varieties are more vigorous than others, and younger trees also tend to require repotting more often. Trident maples and junipers are usually more

vigorous than other species, and they can do with repotting every other year. Other varieties can be left a bit longer before repotting.

Young trees may benefit from repotting every year, while older and more established bonsai may only need repotting every two to three years. Very old specimen trees are repotted once every five to six years.

The best way to tell when a tree needs repotting is to examine the rootball in early spring. If the roots are packed tightly, then it is time to repot. If there are visible spaces between the roots, then

This special tool, which is like a sickle, is used for freeing the rootball from its pot.

The rootball is teased out with this two-pronged fork or root hook.

Make sure all the pot-bound roots are disentangled.

Do not remove more than a third of the roots. Remove about an inch all around to leave room for new soil.

The drainage holes of the container need to be covered with drainage mesh.

If the roots are very pot-bound, disentangle them and cut off the long roots. Cutting roots will not harm a healthy tree.

leave it for another year. Timing is crucial. Early spring is best for most trees. With deciduous trees, watch the dormant buds carefully. The best time to repot is when the buds begin to break, generally in late February to early March. Evergreens are done a month later.

When repotting a bonsai, the rootball is teased out and about a quarter of the roots are cut away to make room for fresh soil to be introduced into the pot. If you simply wish to transfer your bonsai into a larger pot, this may be done at any time of the year, provided the rootball is not disturbed.

Trimming the shoots

A bonsai's shape is maintained by constantly trimming the shoots. A deciduous tree may need to be trimmed up to four to six times a year if it is to be kept in good condition. If trimming is neglected, the tree will very quickly become unkempt. Evergreens, such as pines and junipers, do not need to be trimmed as regularly as deciduous trees.

Use the right ingredients for your soil mix. If in doubt, buy compost from a reputable bonsai nursery.

Mix thoroughly, and sift out dust and very fine particles. Some growers use a layer of coarse drainage material at the bottom of the pot, but this is not strictly necessary.

These wires are for tying the tree in. It is always a good idea to tie in newly planted trees to prevent them from rocking.

Place the tree in the pot, and check that the position and planting angle is right.

Introduce the soil, and make sure that all the holes and crevices are filled by prodding with a chopstick or pencil.

Water in the newly planted tree. If you can use reviving fluid or vitamin B solution, so much the better.

CARE OF INDOOR BONSAI

Most newcomers to bonsai want ones to keep in their living rooms so that they can enjoy them all the time. For those who live in apartments and do not have access to a garden, keeping indoor bonsai is the only possible option. Those keeping indoor bonsai are in the minority, however, as most bonsai are grown outdoors.

Although the purists may argue that there is no such thing as an indoor bonsai, cultivating this form of bonsai may provide more of a challenge than that of keeping hardy, outdoor bonsai. Even if keeping bonsai indoors may be more difficult, the techniques for growing them can be mastered.

Unfortunately, knowledge in this area is a little neglected. Bonsai enthusiasts tend to concentrate on outdoor varieties, with the result that very little information is available on how to grow bonsai indoors. However, with just a little bit of knowledge and lots of patience, it is possible to achieve some measure of success.

Indoor bonsai are tropical and subtropical trees. They are able to survive quite well in the average indoor environment, provided the right type of plant is chosen and the appropriate growing conditions are met. Generally this means giving the plants adequate light, humidity, and warmth. It is important at the outset to distinguish between the two broad types of indoor trees, as they require very different growing conditions.

Tropical varieties, such as the ficus, carmona, and podocarpus, need fairly warm conditions, generally above 60°F in the winter. The subtropical varieties are less likely to require minimum winter temperatures, and some can survive temperatures as low as freezing. In fact, they do not like to be kept too warm in winter, as they need a period of dormancy.

Provided it is understood that subtropical varieties should not be subjected to warm winter conditions and tropical varieties not be allowed to get too cold, there is no reason why these bonsai should

RIGHT: These subtropical Chinese elms are perhaps the most reliable plants for growing indoors.

not grow well indoors. This is why the tropical varieties are referred to as "warm house" plants and the subtropical varieties are known as "cool house" plants.

Tropical varieties include:

Aralia, adenium, carmona, crassula varieties, eugenia, euphorbia, ficus varieties (except F. carica), jacaranda, lantana, malphigia, murraya, podocarpus, sageretia, schefflera, and serissa.

Subtropical varieties include:

Azaleas, Mediterranean box, bougainvillea, camellia, celtis, fraxinus (Chinese ash), fortunella (including all other citrus varieties), gardenia, most fuchsias, crape myrtle, ordinary myrtle, olives, pomegranate, and ulmus or Chinese elm.

The list is by no means comprehensive. Your local bonsai nursery or supplier should be able to recommend what is best for your particular area.

In recent years, the Chinese elm from the subtropical regions of China has been exported to the West in great numbers, making it one of the most popular varieties for indoor bonsai. It is also one of the easiest indoor bonsai to care for. It is extremely hardy and can stand quite a range of indoor conditions. Unlike most of the other indoor bonsai varieties, the Chinese elm can be treated as both an indoor or outdoor subject. When grown indoors, it should be regarded as a subtropical and should therefore be kept cool in winter and allowed to go dormant.

The average European or American living room can seldom replicate the exact humidity and light conditions required for the tropical and subtropical varieties used for indoor bonsai. However, it is possible to create something closely resembling those conditions.

Light is a very important factor for healthy growth. The best position for any indoor subject is on the windowsill or in a conservatory or greenhouse where it gets maximum light. If it is impossible to provide good light, the plant will struggle to survive. Some people go to the trouble of providing special artificial grow lights for their indoor bonsai. This is fine if it can be organized, and the plants will certainly thrive under these conditions. Where light levels are poor and no artificial lighting can be provided, this could be a real problem. Some ficus varieties are able to cope with slightly lower light levels, but even they will eventually succumb to poor health unless better conditions can be given. So, keep your bonsai in as bright a location as possible.

Avoid placing indoor trees on top of radiators, as this can cause them to dry out too quickly. Excessive heat also results in weak, straggly growth. Drafty positions are also detrimental to indoor bonsai. So in winter, make sure that your bonsai are not in cold drafty passageways.

Temperature is clearly an important factor for indoor subjects. Most tropical varieties, or the "warm house" varieties, need a minimum temperature of at least 60°F, but the subtropical varieties, or "cool house" varieties, such as Chinese elm, should be given much cooler winter conditions. Most subtropical varieties need a period of dormancy. If they are made to grow throughout the winter, they will produce unhealthy shoots.

As with most other houseplants, indoor bonsai benefit from being kept outdoors during the summer months. Their condition would improve considerably if this could be done for three or four months each year. There is nothing like fresh air and sunshine to improve a plant's health. If kept indoors all year round, an indoor bonsai's leaves and shoots will become weak.

Water is, of course, the most important requirement of any bonsai, whether it is an indoor or outdoor variety. Remembering to water your tree regularly is extremely important. Make sure that the soil is always moist, but not so wet as to be soggy and waterlogged. Water the soil with a cup of water, letting it drain through into a suitable drip or gravel tray below. You can also water by immersing the pot in a bowl of tepid water. When watering in winter, use water that is at room temperature. Most of the failures with indoor bonsai result from forgetting to water them. If you go away for the weekend or go on vacation, make sure there is someone who will water your tree for you. Some bonsai nurseries provide a plant-sitting service, so ask your local bonsai store or nursery about this.

During the summer you should spray the foliage of your bonsai occasionally to keep the leaves clean and free of dust. You can do this with a hand sprayer or take it outside and wash it down with a garden hose. Like houseplants, indoor trees can also be put in the shower and drenched with tepid water to wash off the dust and grime.

All plants are prone to pests. If you see any pests, such as aphids, white flies, or red spiders, on your bonsai, simply spray it with a garden insecticide at half the recommended strength and leave it to dry. When the pests have been eradicated, you can then clean the leaves with a hand sprayer or garden hose.

All indoor bonsai will need to be fed on a regular basis. You can do this by using a suitable liquid fertilizer. Apply the fertilizer about once every three or four weeks during spring and summer, and in the case of tropical plants, less frequently in winter. For the semitropicals, the feeding program will be slightly different during winter, as these trees go into dormancy at this period; they shouldn't be fed at all at this time. Many of the subtropicals will shed all, if not most, of their leaves in winter. Do not worry if this happens, as the tree is in its dormant state. While it is dormant, the tree should continue to be kept damp, but not too wet. Never let a tree dry out completely, even when it is dormant.

Repotting is necessary once every two to three years for most varieties. You can either repot your tree into a larger pot or simply shake some of the old soil off and replenish with new potting soil. The potting medium for indoor bonsai should be predominantly peat based and not the sticky pond clay that often comes with most of the trees imported from southern China.

Remember to trim the shoots when they get too long, and don't let shoots grow inward. Prune the tree to create the ideal shape and always prune to an outward-pointing bud. A rounded or conical silhouette is what you should be aiming for. Turn the tree at regular intervals, about once a week, so that it faces the light from different sides. By doing this, you will ensure that the tree does not grow

ABOVE: This tropical variety of ficus, Ficus pelkan, *grown by a bonsai enthusiast in New Delhi, has a beautiful root buttress and a good ramification of branches.*

toward the light in one direction and become lopsided.

Conditions in the average living room can never be exactly the same as those in the tropics or subtropics. Although temperature and light levels may approach those in their natural habitats, humidity levels are never the same, because it would be too uncomfortable to live in. Some growers place tropical trees in enclosed glass cases to maintain high humidity levels. This creates an ideal microclimate, but not everyone is willing or able to do this. Compromises are necessary depending on how much you are willing to invest in this hobby.

SEASONAL CARE FOR OUTDOOR BONSAI

Spring

Spring is one of the most colorful seasons in the bonsai calendar. Deciduous trees, which were bare only a few weeks ago, will now be covered with fresh new leaves. Many of the flowering trees will start to blossom, and even the evergreens will put out their new growth in delicate shades of green.

There is such a variety of color, texture, and fragrance during spring. The Japanese maple is a favorite with most bonsai enthusiasts, as it is such a beautiful tree. The red maple is probably the most eye-catching, with its vivid red leaves. There are two particular varieties that have this quality, *Acer palmatum* 'Deshojo' and 'Seigen.' Both are very hardy trees, but must be protected from late spring frosts. If they are left unprotected, their new leaves could be very badly blackened. Spring frosts can also damage the root systems of trident

maples and white pines, especially if they are waterlogged. Keep an eye on weather forecasts at this time of year.

There are many flowering trees that are prominent in spring. The flowering apricot and almond are the first to bloom. Crab apples bloom in late spring, followed closely by wisteria. Nothing could be lovelier than the sight of long racemes of delicate purple, pink, or white wisteria flowers, and it is probably the most heavily scented of all the flowering subjects.

Trees in flower need to be protected from strong sunshine, frost, and rain, but make sure they are watered well to prevent the blossom from prematurely wilting. If you want flowering subjects like crab apple and apricot to set fruit, do not fertilize the tree for about a month after the flowers have fallen.

Some books recommend repotting flowering trees immediately after flowering. This is fine for Satsuki azaleas, but most other flowering trees seem to prefer repotting in the early spring, a month or so before they flower.

LEFT AND ABOVE: Camellia in the informal upright style. It is 35 in. tall, and its trunk is 4¾ in. in diameter.

BONSAI

RIGHT: Japanese red hawthorn reveals its gorgeous blooms in early April.

Summer

Summer is a lovely time to enjoy your bonsai. Watering the trees each day is a relaxing activity. Most of the deciduous bonsai will have their first flush of growth by early summer and need to be kept in good shape by pinching and trimming. Your first priority will be to pinch or trim all the new growth back to one pair of leaves. By doing this, you will eventually give the twigs the dense structure that is typical of exhibition bonsai and those in bonsai manuals. Constant pinching and pruning helps to keep the growth tight and keeps the bonsai from becoming spindly. Over the next few months, continue to pinch or trim until early autumn, and the difference to your deciduous trees will be surprising.

A bonsai cannot remain healthy unless it is fed regularly. Evergreen conifers are normally fed from early spring, starting with a high nitrogen feed and then switching over to a low nitrogen fertilizer in late summer to early autumn.

Deciduous species are treated in much the same way as evergreens, except that feeding is not normally started until the new leaves have hardened. Mature bonsai that have a fine ramification, or very fine, twiggy growth, should be given a much weaker dose of fertilizer. Heavy feeding can induce coarse growth that will spoil the refined look of the tree.

Deciduous trees that have been scorched by hot sun or by inadequate watering can be given a new lease of life by leaf cutting. The new leaves take between three to six weeks to emerge. However, if you wish to experiment with leaf cutting, only do it to healthy, deciduous trees. Bonsai that are not in good health will suffer more damage from leaf cutting than if they were left alone.

BELOW: A mountain maple group has luscious green leaves in early summer.

BELOW: Six months later, the same group has turned a fiery autumn red.

RIGHT: A red hawthorn, Crataegus
oxyacantha *'Paul's Scarlet,' in full
bloom.*

LEFT: Deciduous trees have two flushes of growth—one in early spring, and the other in midsummer. Regular trimming is essential, especially for deciduous trees, to keep your bonsai in shape.

LEFT: Feeding is essential for healthy bonsai. In spring use a high nitrogen feed, while in summer, switch to a low nitrogen fertilizer. The Japanese rapeseed fertilizer is an excellent feed, especially for fruiting and flowering specimens.

RIGHT: Crab apples and hawthorns need to be fed heavily if they are to produce a good crop of flowers and fruit each year. They should also be exposed to full sun.

Autumn

By the end of the summer, heat and drought will have stressed many trees. Maples and other deciduous trees usually suffer scorching, and they often look tired and bedraggled. If you are tempted to prune the leaves, think twice. Leaf pruning in autumn is foolhardy, to say the least. If the leaves on deciduous trees are pruned, any new leaves emerging will certainly be damaged by frost.

What would be beneficial at this time of year is simply an autumn feed to harden the wood for the winter. Leave the scorched leaves on the tree, as they can still provide some nourishment. The best fertilizer to use at this time of year is one that is low in nitrogen (N). Some enthusiasts use a fertilizer that has no nitrogen at all, but this is not strictly necessary. Any fruiting or flowering fertilizer that has a high phosphorous (P) and potassium (K) content is very good. This encourages a rich, autumn color and helps to encourage flower buds next year. Continue to water outdoor trees regularly unless there has been rainfall. Autumn can be dry, so check the soil to see how much water your bonsai needs. Do not let your trees remain waterlogged, as the onset of winter can damage the roots.

Autumn is also a good time to remove wires that are biting into the bark. Pine branches usually thicken in the early autumn, and if wires are not removed in good time, deep scars can form. Although this is not a catastrophe, it can take quite a while for the scars to heal.

RIGHT: Don't be tempted to prune leaves from deciduous trees in the fall, as any subsequent newly emerging leaves could be damaged by winter frosts.

LEFT: A gingko bonsai in late summer. Soon the leaves will turn to gold.

Winter

In cool temperate countries, winter is a fairly quiet time for bonsai. It is, however, a useful time for planning your activities for the year ahead. Temperatures can plummet on very cold nights, so unless you have your trees under cover in a cool greenhouse, make sure they are protected from hard frosts. In some parts of the world where temperatures fall very low, permanent winter homes in protected basements may be the answer. In areas where the average winter temperatures are around 45–50°F, protection in unheated greenhouses is adequate. In colder climates, more sophisticated winter arrangements are certainly worth investing in.

For those who love growing trees from seed, winter is a good time to stratify seeds in readiness for germination in the spring. If you have already purchased your tree seeds, plant them in seed trays now and leave them out to be stratified by the frost. Check what pots, tools, and potting soils you will need for repotting in the spring. Make sure you have the right size pots and soil for the trees that will need to be repotted.

February and March are traditional months for repotting in most temperate regions. Check which of your trees will need to be repotted, and look for when the buds begin to grow to repot them at just the right time.

RIGHT: This winter landscape may look like a Christmas card scene, but the maples here will come to no harm. In an area where winters are not severe, most bonsai can remain outdoors all year round.

HOW TO RESCUE SICK AND DYING TREES

Bonsai trees can sometimes get sick, even if you think you have done all the right things. Fortunately sick trees can be rescued and resuscitated, provided you know what to do. First, you must diagnose the problem.

Trees will suffer if they are neglected. The two most common forms of neglect are waterlogging and dehydration. Both are detrimental to bonsai and will eventually result in the tree dying. Bonsai will die when their roots cannot function properly. Overwatering usually leads to waterlogging, and this will eventually rot the roots. Underwatering, on the other hand, leads to dehydration, and the tree dies from lack of water. In both cases, it is water (or the lack of it) that causes the problem.

Pests and diseases account for far fewer losses than the problems associated with overwatering and underwatering. Forgetting to water bonsai is, of course, a very common mistake, especially for those new to the hobby. Others sometimes kill their trees with kindness by watering them too much. They often stand them in deep saucers or trays of water, which eventually leads to the roots rotting. Taking remedial action before the problem becomes irreversible is crucial if you wish to save your bonsai.

A tree's roots perform two important functions. They draw moisture and nutrients from the soil and they also breathe. If the roots are unable to perform these two functions properly, the tree will get sick and eventually die. In the case of waterlogging, the roots are unable to breathe, while in the case of underwatering, the roots cannot get enough water.

Sick trees that are suffering from overwatering will have blotchy yellow, rather than healthy, green leaves. If you take the rootball out of the pot, there will be no signs of fresh root growth. The root tips will not be white. In fact, most of the roots will be rotten and will smell putrid. The fine roots at the edges of the rootball will be black and will break off at the slightest touch. If there are any signs of life, it will be inside the rootball in the firmer older roots, which are usually more woody and less likely to rot.

Trees that have been allowed to dry out too much will have roots that are completely dry and desiccated. They will no longer be plump and turgid. If there is any chance of survival, the bark of the tree should still be green if the surface of the bark is scratched, and some of the older roots should still be white when scratched.

Reviving a sick tree in both cases involves giving it just enough air and water to bring it back to full health. There are various methods, such as putting sick trees in sharp sand covered with a plastic bag, using pumice, Japanese *akadama*, and also moss peat, but none are entirely satisfactory. By far the best method is to use green sphagnum moss.

The success rate with sphagnum moss is quite astonishing and its use was prompted by the techniques of air layering. When newly rooted air layers are severed from the parent plant, they are immediately potted in pure sphagnum moss. In moss, the new roots develop very rapidly, because there is adequate air and moisture in just the right proportions, added to which are the enzymes and microorganisms in the moss that act symbiotically with the roots to promote root development.

If you have a sick tree whose roots are failing, the first thing to do is to shake most of the old soil off it. If the roots are rotten, then it might pay to hose off all the stale soil, cut off all the dead and rotten roots, and then place it in a deep flower pot filled with fresh sphagnum moss. Use a bit of root reviver and keep the sick patient in a shady but humid atmosphere. Make sure the moss is always damp but not soaking wet. New roots should form in 3–4 weeks. This can be done at any time of the year, but the best results are in the spring and summer. If done in autumn or winter, the tree will not die, but will be slow in producing new roots. New roots will form quickly during spring.

When new roots have formed, you can add bonsai potting soil gradually around the edges of the pot and also introduce some general fertilizer. In a few months, your sick tree will have recovered completely.

RIGHT: This sick juniper is well on its way to full health using the sphagnum moss treatment. New roots have already filled the pot.

This method is also useful when trees have been in pots for too long, and the soil has become hard and compacted, making it difficult for the roots to breathe. By simply teasing out the old soil and putting the rootball in a basket of pure sphagnum moss, the sick tree will soon revive. In just a few weeks, the sick tree will be rejuvenated, but do not rush to put it back in its pot right away. Leave it to recover until the following spring, and it will then be ready for reinstating back in its original pot using new bonsai potting soil.

RIGHT: Japanese maples can sometimes get very sick and weak if left pot-bound for too long. By using the sphagnum moss trick, sick trees can be revived very quickly.

BELOW: Sphagnum moss certainly induces new roots to form quickly. This is the rootball of the Chinese juniper shown on the opposite page.

Chapter 3 – Creating Your Own Bonsai

Most bonsai enthusiasts derive great pleasure from creating and training their own bonsai. Those with a little more patience start with seedlings and cuttings, others may use established nursery trees and shrubs, and the more adventurous may try their hand at very large material.

SEEDLINGS AND CUTTINGS

This is a relatively slow process, but is very rewarding if you enjoy growing things. All bonsai start this way, but the techniques used by commercial growers are quite different from those used by the amateur. Commercial growers develop young plants under intensive growing conditions and train them into bonsai when the trunks have reached a reasonable size. Most amateurs develop their bonsai in pots from a very early stage, which is a much slower process.

If you wish to grow bonsai from seed, use fresh seed or pregerminated seed for the best results. Bonsai seed kits are no more than ordinary tree seeds packaged with some potting soil. Seeds from reputable seed companies are a far better value. Remember too that some seeds are easier to germinate than others. Most hard-coated seeds will require stratification to break their dormancy. So follow the seed sowing instructions carefully.

Once the seedlings germinate, they should not be wired or shaped until they are at least a couple of years old. Seedlings should be potted into individual pots to develop into strong plants. Pinch out the growing tip when three or four pairs of leaves have formed. This will encourage bushiness. Shaping and wiring can commence when the stem is at least about as thick as a matchstick. Do not be in too great a hurry to pot them into bonsai pots.

Cuttings should be treated in very much the same way as seedlings. Let them grow into strong plants before shaping. Most varieties of trees and shrubs are suitable for bonsai, so experiment with anything that appeals to you.

RIGHT: These six-year-old silver birch and larch are already 19 in. high.

BELOW: Five needle pines are easy to grow from seed. These are newly germinated.

VARIETIES TO LOOK FOR

You can use trees and shrubs for making bonsai. Deciduous trees that are suitable for bonsai include flowering cherries, hawthorn, crab apple, maples, beech, hornbeam, and even fruiting trees. Choose the bush form rather than standards and half standards. Deciduous trees may take longer to develop, but they will reward you with changes in color and form as the seasons change.

If the trees are grafted, make sure that the graft is fairly low. Many conifers are also suitable, and these include most pines, junipers, chamaecyparis (but not Lawsons), cedars, and cryptomerias.

Many shrubs are ideal subjects for bonsai. Cotoneaster, pyracantha, potentilla, miniature roses, berberis, and many of the dwarf conifers are just some of the varieties suitable for bonsai.

NURSERY AND GARDEN CENTER MATERIAL

If you don't want to bother with seedlings and cuttings, then nursery plants are the answer. They are a quick and instant source of bonsai material, provided you go about it the right way.

There is a bewildering range of species and sizes to choose from, so look for plants that have an interesting shape, a thick trunk, small leaves, and if relevant, small fruit or flowers.

Don't worry if they appear to be a bit pot-bound, as repotting will soon rejuvenate them. You can shape the trunk and branches at any time of the year, but remember that any drastic root pruning should be left until the dormant season, or better still, until early spring.

BASIC TECHNIQUES

There are two basic ways of making bonsai. You can either grow a young seedling or cutting to the appropriate size, or cut down a larger and more mature tree to the size you want. Each method has its advantages and drawbacks.

Growing bonsai from seedlings and cuttings is a slow process, but the results can be more refined. The cutting-down method is a quicker approach but can leave unsightly scars if not done properly. When using seedlings and cuttings, constant pinching and pruning of the growing shoots will eventually produce a tree that resembles a bonsai. Wiring and shaping selected branches later on will create a more refined bonsai shape. Aim for a conical shape with adequate spacing between branches.

Young trees in training may benefit from repotting every year (see Chapter One: Repotting or trimming the roots).

ABOVE: Most Japanese five needle pine bonsai are grafted onto black pine rootstock. These are newly grafted plants.

RIGHT: Young maples at Herons Bonsai, Surrey, England.

TOOLS AND ACCESSORIES

Shaping is achieved by cutting and bending the trunks and branches. With copper or aluminum wire, trunks and branches can be bent to the required shape. Most bonsai nurseries stock a bewildering range of tools and accessories for making bonsai, each with a very specific use. If you are just starting in the hobby, there are probably only a few tools that are essential: long-handled trimming scissors, a concave branch cutter, root pruning scissors, and a rake for teasing out roots. Ordinary pruning shears and wire cutters are also very useful.

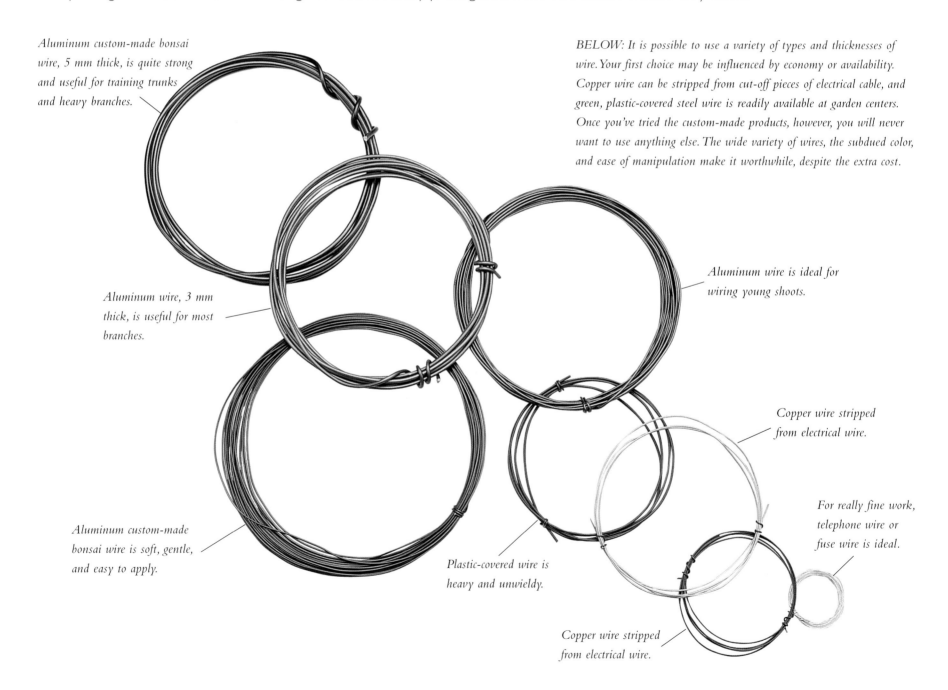

Aluminum custom-made bonsai wire, 5 mm thick, is quite strong and useful for training trunks and heavy branches.

Aluminum wire, 3 mm thick, is useful for most branches.

Aluminum custom-made bonsai wire is soft, gentle, and easy to apply.

BELOW: It is possible to use a variety of types and thicknesses of wire. Your first choice may be influenced by economy or availability. Copper wire can be stripped from cut-off pieces of electrical cable, and green, plastic-covered steel wire is readily available at garden centers. Once you've tried the custom-made products, however, you will never want to use anything else. The wide variety of wires, the subdued color, and ease of manipulation make it worthwhile, despite the extra cost.

Aluminum wire is ideal for wiring young shoots.

Copper wire stripped from electrical wire.

For really fine work, telephone wire or fuse wire is ideal.

Plastic-covered wire is heavy and unwieldy.

Copper wire stripped from electrical wire.

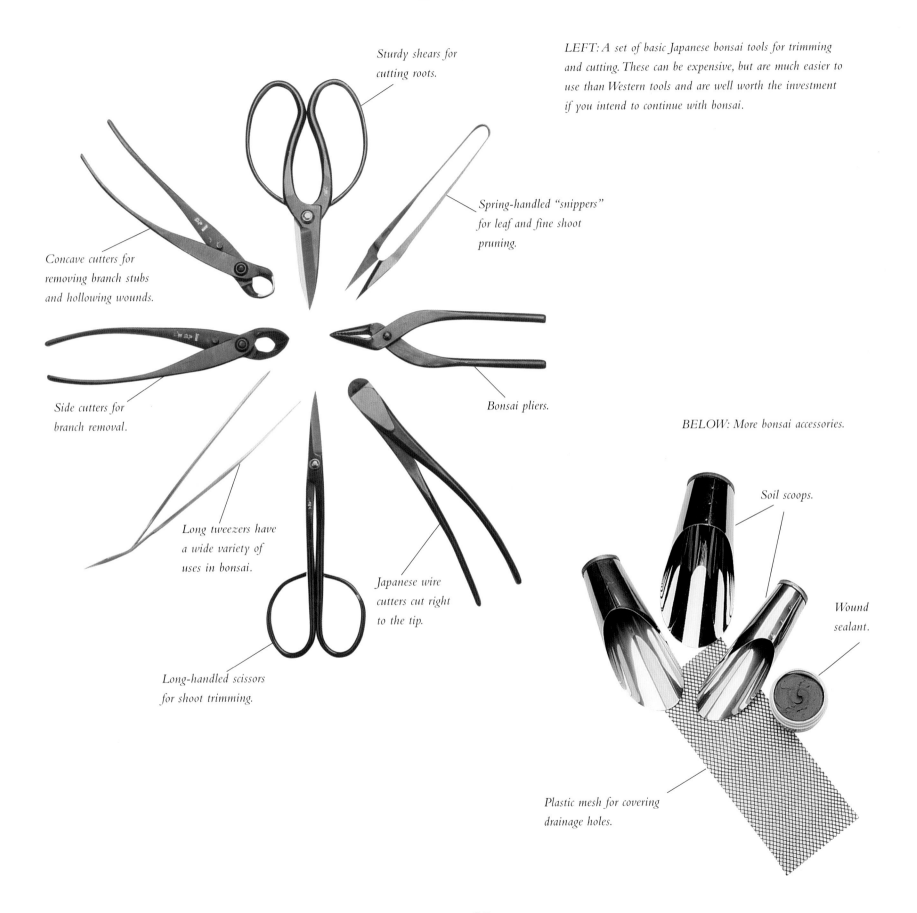

Sturdy shears for cutting roots.

LEFT: A set of basic Japanese bonsai tools for trimming and cutting. These can be expensive, but are much easier to use than Western tools and are well worth the investment if you intend to continue with bonsai.

Spring-handled "snippers" for leaf and fine shoot pruning.

Concave cutters for removing branch stubs and hollowing wounds.

Side cutters for branch removal.

Bonsai pliers.

BELOW: More bonsai accessories.

Long tweezers have a wide variety of uses in bonsai.

Japanese wire cutters cut right to the tip.

Soil scoops.

Wound sealant.

Long-handled scissors for shoot trimming.

Plastic mesh for covering drainage holes.

PINCHING FOR PERFECTION

Pinching is one of the regular tasks in bonsai. It involves nipping young soft shoots back with your fingers or tweezers in order to control unwanted growth. A tedious chore perhaps, but a very essential one for keeping bonsai in good shape. Nipping with the fingers is better than using scissors, because scissors will leave brown marks on the foliage of evergreens such as juniper and cryptomeria.

Pinching should be done regularly throughout the growing season. Most trees have two bursts of growth: the first is in early spring and the second in midsummer. Pinching is particularly important during these periods.

With deciduous trees, such as beech, maple, hornbeam, or elm, you can pinch using your fingernails or tweezers. As soon as the shoots start to elongate, they should be pinched. Try not to allow the new shoots to extend to more than three or four pairs of

leaves. If this happens, then you have let the tree go too far. Trim back to one pair of leaves and keep it under control. By constantly pinching the new shoots, you will create a fine ramification or dense twig structure, which is the ideal to aim for when creating a bonsai.

If you wish to develop your bonsai into a larger size, leave the shoots to grow to the desired height and width, and then trim back. Constantly pinching from then on will produce fuller foliage and keep it at that size. Remember to leave spaces between alternate branches by trimming off shoots that are growing directly above or below the branch line. Also avoid branches that cross or are ingrowing.

Continue to feed at regular intervals, usually about once a month, but take care not to give mature trees, and those that do not need further development, excessive fertilizer. For mature bonsai, a weak feed is all that is needed.

Throughout the growing season, you will need to keep a close eye on any pests or diseases that may attack the tree. As soon as they appear, spray with pesticide or fungicide.

LEFT: Junipers are prone to scale insect infestation. Spray with insecticide as soon as the pests appear.

RIGHT: The fine ramification on this massive Japanese maple, 35 in. high and 3 ft. wide, has been achieved by years of constant pinching. This is the author's favorite bonsai and has been in his collection since 1976.

LEAF PRUNING

There is a great deal of mystique surrounding the pruning of leaves for bonsai. The subject fascinates most bonsai enthusiasts, but few understand the reason for doing it, and even fewer are able to do it properly. Not all bonsai are suitable for this treatment.

Leaf pruning is the process of removing the leaves on deciduous trees in order to induce a crop of new leaves in the same growing season. This is best done in early summer and should not be done later than late summer. If it is done too late, the new leaves may not mature sufficiently before autumn.

When leaf pruning, every leaf should be removed, as a partial removal may not encourage new leaves to emerge from the defoliated branches. Leaf pruning is usually carried out on Japanese maples and trident maples. The very dense and small-leafed varieties, such as 'Kiyohime' and 'Kashima,' are the usual subjects for leaf pruning, while ordinary mountain maple and trident maple are also sometimes given this treatment.

There are two main reasons for leaf pruning. The first is to enable light and air to penetrate the very dense, twiggy structure of certain varieties of bonsai, and the second is to produce a finer crop of slightly smaller leaves. Leaf pruning is sometimes performed on trees that have been badly scorched by the sun or inadvertently allowed to dry out. It enables them to generate new leaves, so that they can produce the carbohydrates needed to sustain growth.

In Japanese bonsai nurseries, the very dense and small-leafed maples that are usually grown in the broom style are pruned in early summer. The

leaf pruning is done so that light can penetrate the very dense structure of twigs. If these trees were left to their own devices, the dense branches would soon die from insufficient light. Leaf pruning is therefore a means of maintaining vigor in this particular species of tree. It is seldom done to reduce the size of the leaves, as the reduction in size will only be marginal. However, the color of the second crop of leaves is usually better and is considered to be the main advantage of performing this technique.

Leaf pruning should never be performed on trees that are in poor health, as they may not have the energy to put out new growth. Indigenous trees tend to respond well to leaf pruning, as they are usually much more robust. In Europe, varieties such as sycamore, horse chestnut, beech, and hornbeam are ideal subjects for this treatment.

LEFT AND ABOVE: These Kashima maples have just been leaf pruned in mid-June.
A new crop of leaves should appear in 3–4 weeks.

JUNIPERUS
CHINENSIS

DISPLAYING BONSAI

LEFT: An ancient Chinese juniper belonging to the author on show at the world famous Chelsea Flower Show, England. The bonsai is displayed in a traditional tokonoma *complete with scroll painting and* suiseki.

Once you have a nice collection of trees, they should be displayed properly so that you get the maximum enjoyment from them. Most growers display their bonsai on benches in the garden or on the patio where they can be seen and enjoyed from the house.

With the increase in crime in recent years, it is a good idea to have some security measures in your back garden to deter any opportunistic thieves. A strong lock on garden gates and a security alarm system are good deterrents against the unfortunate removal of your valuable bonsai and will put your mind more at ease.

If you need further inspiration on how to display your bonsai, most of the major flower shows throughout the world exhibit them.

At the annual Chelsea Flower Show in England, there are usually seven or eight stands displaying bonsai to eager visitors.

Many clubs also put on their own shows from time to time, and these usually take place in the summer. Look for advertisements in local newspapers or newsletters that tell you what is going on in your area.

Most botanical gardens and arboretums also have permanent bonsai collections, and these are certainly inspiring and worth visiting if you are a bonsai lover.

LEFT: Slatted benches are ideal for displaying your bonsai collection.

BONSAI POTS

No bonsai is complete without a suitable pot. After all, a bonsai is by definition a tree in a pot. Choosing the right pot is an art. Not only must the pot be the right size, but its shape, texture, and color have an important bearing on the final appearance of the bonsai.

There are many rules and conventions for choosing pots, but as a general guide, use rectangular pots for the more powerful looking trees, such as those with heavy trunks. These are usually in the formal upright, slanting, or driftwood styles. Tall pots are used for bonsai in the cascade style (see Chapter One). Oval and round pots are generally used for trees with more delicate trunks and branches.

The pot should suit the species of tree as well as its style. Pines, junipers, and trident maples with thick trunks look best growing out of deep rectangular or oval pots, whereas mountain maples and Japanese gray bark elms look more elegant in shallow oval and round pots.

When buying bonsai pots, especially those made by local potters, make sure that there is adequate drainage. There should be at least one or two large drainage holes. Pots for outdoor bonsai should be made of stoneware clay, if they are to be frostproof.

BELOW: *A* mame *pot, although tiny, is similar in shape and quality to the full-sized pots. Mame pots tend to be more colorful.*

RIGHT: *Sturdy, cream-based ovals like this one look good with maples and elms. They are too delicate for strong conifer arrangements.*

RIGHT: *The subtle gray-green glaze on this elegant rectangle would suit most broad-leaved species and styles, and could look good with informal upright larches too.*

ABOVE: *Very shallow oval glazed pot, designed specifically for group plantings.*

ABOVE: *Standard brown, unglazed Kobi-ware rectangle. If in doubt, this type of pot will do for almost anything.*

PREVIOUS PAGE AND RIGHT: *Just some of the many pots at Herons Nursery, Surrey, England. These are Japanese pots from the Tokoname region.*

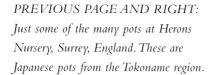

LEFT: *This shallow, elegant, round pot in a gentle, unglazed gray would suit delicate styles, such as literati, or deciduous clumps with thin trunks.*

LEFT: *Strong, flared, unglazed rectangle suitable for heavy-trunked conifers, especially driftwood types.*

ABOVE: *The drum style pot is made in a variety of sizes and is best used for strong-trunked literati or formal upright styles. It could also be successfully used for heavy clumps.*

Chapter 4 – Advanced Techniques

BONSAI FROM SEED

Many people are introduced to bonsai through bonsai seed kits, which usually contain a few tree seeds and a bag of soil. Disillusionment soon follows, when they discover that their bonsai kit does not produce the beautiful bonsai shown on the packaging. Most likely they will get an ordinary tree, which if left to grow, would make a reasonable nursery specimen.

However, it is possible to grow bonsai from seed with the right materials and information. Seed kits can be fun, but the seeds

themselves must be fresh and viable if they are to germinate successfully. If seeds are stale, the chances of germination are reduced. All seeds have a shelf life, and if they have been stored in the wrong conditions for too long, they will not be viable.

Most hard-coated seeds germinate more readily if stratified in a freezer or left in a seed tray outside in winter. The repeated freezing and thawing helps to break the dormancy of the seeds. Some firms now sell pregerminated seeds, which take a lot of the guesswork out of seed sowing. Raising seedlings, however, is only the first step in making bonsai. The young seedlings will need a lot of training and shaping over the following several years if they are to resemble the real thing.

Growing bonsai from seeds is a relatively slow process. There are easier ways of creating bonsai, such as using ordinary nursery material or field-grown trees. Bonsai can also be produced from cuttings, and even hedging material. All plants and trees have the potential to be made into bonsai, but some varieties are more suitable than others. Suitable varieties are those that have small leaves or fine foliage. Japanese maple and Japanese gray bark elm are favorites, while in the U.K., species such as field maple, English elm,

LEFT AND NEXT PAGE: Wisteria are easy to grow from seed. Collect the seeds in the fall, leave them out over winter in seed trays to stratify, and they will germinate in spring.

ABOVE: This bonsai nursery in Japan produces everything from young plants to mature specimens.

LEFT: These young maple seedlings were grown from seeds collected by the author in Kyoto the previous fall.

beech, hornbeam, cotoneaster, hawthorn, juniper, larch, Scots pine, and yew are all very suitable material.

There is, of course, no such thing as special bonsai seed. Tree seeds are tree seeds, and the seedlings that germinate will become ordinary trees if left untrained. Seedlings need to be grown for at least two to three years before any training should be done. Small seedlings are ideal for making smaller bonsai, and beautiful little trees from 2 to 3 in. high can be created simply by repeatedly clipping the growing points. This makes the twig structure dense in a relatively short space of time. Japanese gray bark elm and Japanese maple respond well to this treatment.

In three to four years you can make lovely *shohin*, or small, bonsai that can even be displayed at exhibitions. Larger and older looking bonsai are more difficult to create from seed in a short time. A different approach is needed here. The most common method is to grow the seedlings in open ground for a few years until the trunks are thick enough for the size of bonsai desired. The trees are then reduced in height and the branches allowed to regrow again.

If you want to train seedlings into traditional bonsai S shapes using wire, they are best left until they are at least two to three years old. Newly emerged seedlings should be pricked out into individual pots and grown until they are 4–5 in. high. They should then be potted into slightly larger pots, in order to encourage strong and bushy growth. Regularly pinching the growth points will achieve this. If seedlings are not pinched at the tips, they will become leggy and won't develop a dense branch structure.

If you wish to make a larger bonsai, you will need to plant it in open ground or in a flower bed. When it has thickened up sufficiently, it can be dug up and put in a bonsai pot for final training. It is a mistake to transfer young seedlings that are less than a couple of years old into bonsai pots. Seedlings should only be put into bonsai pots when the trunks are woody and have some character.

RIGHT: A four-year-old Scots pine seedling is trained into the literati style. This style is reminiscent of ancient pines, which tend to shed their lower branches as they get old. The focal point of the design is the trunk, which needs to have a lot of character.

FIELD GROWING TECHNIQUES

There is absolutely no substitute for field growing if you want to make a large bonsai in a relatively short space of time. It is a quick and reliable way of producing a thick trunk and a good taper to the shape of the tree in just a few years. Although different species have different rates of growth, they will all thicken much faster if grown in the ground than if cultivated in pots or containers. Japanese and Chinese bonsai growers use this method for commercial production to cut down considerably on growing time and make bonsai more financially viable. In Japan, where there is still a fairly big bonsai industry, growers set aside vast fields for mass producing most of the popular varieties used in bonsai, such as maple, white pine, and black pine.

The techniques used for the commercial growing of bonsai can be adopted by amateurs, too. Growing trees in the ground is great fun, saves a lot of time, and produces stunning results. You can start at any stage by planting one- or two-year-old seedlings, or trees and shrubs that are already a few years old. A big field in which to practice the open ground technique is not a necessity; you can use a bit of your garden or herbaceous border to achieve the same results. The tree needs to be left in the ground for at least two full growing seasons to develop the desired thickness of trunk.

Once a tree has been planted in the ground, it will soon take root and grow quickly. Shoots could grow 3 ft. or more each year, depending on the species and growing conditions. English field maple, hornbeam, Scots pine, larch, and elm are all extremely vigorous species. A one-year-old sapling, which may be ⅛ in. in diameter to begin with, could become ½ in. thick in its third year, growing eventually to 3–4 in. in diameter by its seventh or eighth year. One English field maple, which began with a 1 in. thick trunk, became an amazing 15 in. in diameter after several years and three or four transplants.

In the initial growth period, it is best to leave the tree undisturbed for four or five years. Do not prune any of the top growth or undercut the roots. Left to grow without any interference, it will reach 10–12 ft., depending on the species. In the fourth or fifth year, the tree can be cut down to 2 ft. and then lifted from the ground. The thick roots should be trimmed back to 4–6 in., leaving as much of the fine feeder roots as possible.

If the tree is thick enough for your purposes, then you can start to develop the taper. This is best achieved by cutting the tree down to the point where you want the taper to begin and then planting the tree back into the ground. Many Japanese growers do this by making an initial horizontal cut across the trunk to minimize the surface area exposed and to reduce transpiration. A sloping cut

RIGHT: New leaders from trident maples are left to grow to ensure that the trunk is tapered. When the leaders are no longer needed, the air-layering technique is used to produce more trees.

RIGHT: Interesting-looking roots that show on the surface are essential for a top-quality bonsai. The roots give the trunk a lot of character.

PREVIOUS PAGE: The author with one of his field-grown pines.

exposes a greater surface area and is more likely to cause the tree to die back. There is no guarantee that a new leader will emerge from the tip of the point of the sloping cut anyway. The chances are that the new leader will sprout from somewhere else and all your efforts could be wasted.

Producing the desired taper to the top of the tree is a much longer and more tedious process. It involves repeatedly growing and cutting back the current year's leader. With trident maples, each year's leader needs to grow 10 ft. before it is cut back to 1 in.

This process is repeated year after year until you get the desired taper and height for your bonsai. The branches are unimportant at this stage. You can encourage the lower branches to grow and even let some of them grow unchecked for several years to serve as "sacrificial" branches later on. These branches will help the trunk thicken and create the desirable flare to the base of the trunk.

Do not let too many branches grow from the area where a taper is required to prevent a lump from forming and losing the gradual tapering effect. This effect can be seen on pollarded trees, such as plane and lime, where lumps form in the area where branches have been cut.

If you wish to develop a buttress for the roots, or a "turtle back" root, try placing a brick or roof tile under the tree when you plant the tree back in the ground after its first lifting. This will force the roots to spread sideways and create the classic plate-root effect.

There is not a lot that needs to be done to the tree while it is growing in the ground, apart from feeding it occasionally with a general fertilizer. Water the tree when it is first planted, and make sure it does not dry out while it is getting established in its first year. Do not attempt to lift the tree from the ground until it has had at least three or four growing seasons. If it gets too tall, chop the top off to a manageable height, or chop it down to

LEFT AND OPPOSITE: Trees grown at a nursery in open ground are lifted in the early spring. A mechanical digger makes light work of lifting.

start developing the taper. Do not worry about the taproot when it is in the ground. It can be severed when the tree is lifted.

At Herons Bonsai nursery, when the field grown trees have reached the requisite size and have a decent taper, they are lifted from the ground with a mechanical digger. The roots are trimmed, and in the case of deciduous trees, all the branches are cut off. They are then potted in 13–25 gallon pots or large boxes ready for styling and training into bonsai. They are potted up using a fairly sandy mix that is half loam and half sand. This mix usually induces fine roots.

Japanese growers use river sand for potting large trident maple stumps. The roots that emerge by using this potting medium are quite astonishing. When just sand is used as the potting medium, a heavy feeding program is necessary. A good general fertilizer or high nitrogen fertilizer in the spring makes a good start, followed by rapeseed fertilizer in the late summer.

Once trees are potted, spend time developing the branches into the desired style. If things go according to plan, it is possible to create a decent specimen tree from field material in as little as three years. The transition from training pot to the first bonsai pot could be within one year, depending on how quickly the roots have developed. If a much shallower pot is needed, then a longer wait is necessary, as the rootball may have to be reduced in several stages before it can be transferred to a pot.

British species such as hornbeam, English field maple, beech, elm, and Scots pine are all fairly resilient. They stand up to root pruning pretty well and are not susceptible to cold and frost.

Large specimens of these particular varieties are easy to make in a relatively short space of time when compared with other bonsai. You will see the results of all your efforts almost certainly within your lifetime and with many years to spare.

LARGE BONSAI – SOME SUITABLE VARIETIES

Seeing a large bonsai can bring about the same emotions as listening to a great piece of music or seeing a beautiful sunset. Many bonsai enthusiasts love the larger bonsai, although there are some who don't. Of all the species, there is certainly nothing that can beat the trident maple as a large bonsai.

Unfortunately, large bonsai are generally more expensive than smaller ones. Owning a large bonsai can be an expensive business, unless you can make them yourself from relatively inexpensive material. Most indigenous trees grow at a very fast rate, given the right conditions. In temperate countries, varieties such as hornbeam, beech, maple, larch, and elm can grow at a phenomenal rate if planted in the ground for five or six years. If trained properly, they can be made into superb specimens in fewer than ten years. Similarly, in the tropics, most ficus, bougainvillea, elms, carmonas, murraya, celtis, and a host of other varieties grow at a phenomenal rate, and they are all highly suitable for making into large bonsai.

Large trunk specimens are created in three basic stages. The first stage is simply to let the tree grow unchecked for ten, twenty, or even thirty years, perhaps lifting them occasionally to cut the roots to make them easier to lift at a later date. The second stage is to cut the tree down to 1–2 ft. from the ground and grow the leader again to achieve a reasonable taper. The third stage is to cut all the branches back to the main trunk and then grow them again for the final shape.

Commercial bonsai nurseries, especially those in Japan and Korea, export thick stumps that have trunk diameters ranging from 8 to 20 in. Some are well tapered and are almost complete bonsai, except for the branches, while others still have a long way to go before they can be called classics.

Trident maples are a good example of this type of material as they are quick-growing trees. A good trident maple with a 15–20 in. diameter trunk is usually only twenty or thirty years old. Repeated cutting of successive leaders will develop the taper until a desired shape is achieved. With only a few years refinement, all the branches can be shaped into a perfect specimen.

Heavy pruning of the branches is best done in the summer, because healing and callusing of the wounds occurs much faster than if performed in the winter. By applying cut paste to the exposed surfaces, callusing can be speeded up even more rapidly. If you wish to create holes and hollows in the trunk, then simply leave the cut surfaces exposed, and in time, the wood will rot in that spot, leaving very natural-looking holes and crevices in the trunk.

Once the taper has reached a reasonable stage of development, the final choice and development of branches can begin. Don't leave the wires on the branches for more than a couple of months during the growing season, as the branches can scar badly if left unchecked. In a single growing season, you may have to rewire the branches two or three times if you wish to avoid leaving wire marks on the branches. An alternative method of training the branches is to simply guy them down, instead of wiring in the conventional way.

A ten-year program of development is a reasonable timescale for achieving a perfect specimen. Nothing can be more satisfying than seeing the results of your handiwork on such a grand scale.

ABOVE: Cuts from heavy pruning in the summer will heal and callus over quickly.

OPPOSITE: This exquisite trident maple, 51 in. across and 43 in. high, with a root base of 15¾ in. wide, was created from air layering in Japan forty years ago. It forms part of the author's collection.

AIR LAYERING

Air layering is a method of propagation in which mature branches are used to produce a newly rooted plant. It has been used as a method for general plant propagation in the East for many centuries. It is still in common use today in India, China, Japan, and throughout southeast Asia, both in general plant nurseries and for bonsai. When used for bonsai, the advantages are obvious, as a fully formed tree can be produced in a matter of months.

Air layering saves time, and for bonsai growers, it certainly makes a lot of commercial sense. Gardeners and horticulturists in the West are not familiar with this method, and for many it is an alien technique. Bonsai enthusiasts, however, have come to realize the benefits of air layering, and many now use it with great success.

There are certain species of tree where air layering can be used very easily. Japanese maples, beech, hornbeam, willow, juniper, and wisteria are good examples. Air layerings taken from early spring to midsummer will root in a matter of weeks, and Japanese maples, for example, can root in as little as three weeks. Most deciduous trees will air layer easily, and evergreen conifers can be just as obliging.

The technique involves cutting away a ring of bark from the portion of branch you wish to air layer. There are many variations of the technique. Sometimes you can leave a sliver of bark to act as a bridge or you may tie a ring of wire to restrict the flow of sap. By trial and error you can experiment with different methods to find the one best suited to you.

When you air layer a tree, use a branch that has the most character. Select one that has a nice curve and good taper. Such a branch will be preferable to one that is simply straight and parallel. Trees that are vigorous can, in fact, be shaped while still attached to the parent plant. By careful selection, you can train and style branches into any desired shape in a matter of weeks.

Starting from virtually nothing, it is possible to create a fully formed bonsai, complete with all the desired characteristics, such as a beautifully shaped and tapered trunk and properly placed branches, in just one growing season.

ABOVE: Remove a ring of bark with a sharp knife.

ABOVE: Wrap a ball of sphagnum moss around the area that has been cut.

RIGHT: Bubble wrap is a good medium for holding everything in place, as it retains warmth and allows you to see when the roots have formed.

BONSAI

Chapter 5 – Popular Varieties

PINES

Pines are always an enigma to anyone new to bonsai. You either love them or hate them. They are lovely to look at as bonsai, but difficult to come to grips with if you are starting from scratch. You do need to have some knowledge of pines to be able to grow and care for them properly and achieve successful results.

To the uninitiated, a young, untrained pine is not exactly the most attractive looking plant, as it tends to look like a bottlebrush. The foliage or needles are stiff and ungainly, and are extremely difficult to handle. As for creating foliage pads, this would be a daunting task for the novice. But once you get hooked on pines, you will not want to grow anything else. In Japan, the black pine is often considered the "king of bonsai," while its counterpart, the white pine, is referred to as its consort or "queen." Pines are certainly the favorite species for most connoisseurs of bonsai.

Suitable species of pine

Pines are widely spread throughout the world. Most varieties of pines grow in the temperate zone, although there are some that grow in the warm tropics. They are known as one needle, two

RIGHT: Specimen pines.

OPPOSITE: Pines can be difficult for beginners, but once hooked, you won't want to grow anything else. Look at expertly trained bonsai pines, such as this, for inspiration.

LEFT: *The bark on an old Scots pine bonsai makes this a fine specimen.*

RIGHT: *The cork bark of a Japanese black pine shows a lot of character.*

BOTTOM: *Detail showing the needles of a Japanese black pine.*

OPPOSITE: *Japanese five needle pine in the informal upright style.*

needle, three needle, and five needle pines, where the needles grow in bunches of one, two, three, or five, respectively. Pines can vary enormously in character. Some have smooth bark, others rough bark; some have long needles, some short needles.

Their growth habits can be extremely diverse, too. There are dwarf and prostrate varieties; others grow very straight, and a few have very contorted trunks. Most varieties can be used for bonsai, although some are clearly more suitable than others.

In China, Korea, and Japan, the five needle pine, *Pinus parviflora*, or *goyo matsu*, and the black pine, *Pinus thunbergii*, or *kuro matsu*, are the most widely used species for bonsai and garden trees. The red pine, *Pinus densiflora*, or *aka matsu*, is not so often seen, but when it is used for bonsai, it is mainly for the *bunjin*, or literati style.

The five needle, or white, pine derives its name from the white line down the middle of each needle, which gives the tree a whitish gray appearance. The black pine has dark green needles and a very dark, almost black trunk. The red pine is very similar to the Scots pine, with a reddish brown bark that makes it an attractive specimen.

RIGHT: Japanese five needle pine on black pine rootstock. The yellowing needles appear early in the fall.

LEFT: Pine needles can be stiff and ungainly to handle, but pine bonsai are still a favorite species for connoisseurs.

The Asiatic pines are all very strong trees for bonsai in their native habitats, but in the West, they need to be handled more carefully to get the best results. The Japanese five-needle, or white, pine has been imported into Europe and America for many years. It is grown quite extensively as bonsai and as garden trees all over Japan. The majority, however, are grown in southern Japan where the climate is warm and almost subtropical. Some are grown in the north, which has a much cooler temperature and is very similar to northern Europe.

Pines from the warmer southern regions of Japan, such as 'Shikoku,' 'Takamatsu,' or 'Kyushu,' may not be entirely hardy when imported into Europe and North America. They can be vulnerable to the cold in severe winter conditions. Consequently, white pines imported from southern Japan will require some winter protection.

Pines that originate from the middle and northern regions of Japan tend to be hardier and are probably more suited to American conditions because they originate from a cooler climate. It is important to remember, however, that all imported pines from Japan need some degree of winter protection.

Pines and other conifers from China, Korea, or Japan are subject to very stringent import restrictions in the U.S., as in most other countries. The white pine, *Pinus parviflora*, from Japan, can often only be imported with a license. The black pine, *Pinus thunbergii*, and the red pine, *Pinus densiflora*, are totally banned in some countries as a precaution against the introduction of foreign pests and plant diseases. It is advisable to seek the advice of the appropriate government department before bringing any plant material home.

In Europe, there are many species and varieties of pine that are suitable for bonsai. The Scots pine, *Pinus sylvestris*, the mugo pine, *Pinus mugo*, the shore pine, *Pinus contorta*, and the Austrian black pine, *Pinus nigra*, are all very suitable for bonsai work. They are extremely hardy, too. Most of these species have their cultivars, which very often are even more suitable for bonsai, because they either have very short needles, or interesting trunks.

The Scots pine 'Beuvronensis,' for instance, is a dwarf variety with a very dense habit and lovely short needles. Similarly, the mugo pine has a vast array of cultivars, such as 'Humpy,' 'Mops,' and 'Pumillo,' that are all suitable for bonsai. The same is true for *Pinus nigra*.

The variety 'Hornibrookiana' is particularly good for bonsai as it strongly resembles the Japanese black pine. All the European pines are extremely hardy when grown as bonsai and need no winter protection. They can even survive temperatures as low as 10°F.

General care

All pines are fairly easy to care for, though the Japanese pines will require some winter protection and more careful handling when repotting. The European pines do not need such special treatment.

Soil

Most pines will grow in almost any medium, although an open, gritty mix is probably best. In Japan, pines from the warmer south are usually potted in pure river sand, while those which are grown in the Tokyo area and further north are potted in a special soil called *akadama*.

Akadama is a warmer soil suitable for colder areas, whereas sand tends to be much colder in winter and holds more moisture in the warmer Japanese winter. In the central regions of Japan, they use a combination of the two, which is a mix consisting of forty percent sand and sixty percent *akadama*. This mix would be suitable for all pines grown in Europe and America.

ABOVE: Needles of the Japanese black pine.

OPPOSITE: Pinus sylvestris beuvronensis *is a very versatile type of Scots pine. It can be trained into any style from cascade, as it is here, to even the raft or clump style.*

Repotting

Pines are best repotted in mid to late spring. This applies to all pines, whether they are European or Japanese. They generally do not require repotting more than once every two or three years, and for older specimens, once every four or five years. It is best not to prune the roots too much when repotting; taking off about a fifth is plenty. With imported Japanese white pines, you should take even less off, as they are very sensitive to root disturbance.

Most of the casualties with white pines are the result of overly enthusiastic root pruning. After repotting, pines benefit from being kept in a humid environment for a couple of weeks to stimulate the production of new roots. Mist them regularly to maintain the humid atmosphere. Do not keep newly potted trees in the humid area longer than is necessary, as sudden warm spells can dehydrate them completely. After repotting them, a dose of plant reviver or root developer will help their recovery.

Seasonal care

Although pines are evergreen conifers, they do have to shed their old needles from time to time, usually in the autumn. If a Scots or Japanese white pine starts shedding handfuls of needles, don't panic. This is perfectly normal. All that needs to be done is to clean the yellow needles off the tree and the pine will look as good as new.

Unlike deciduous trees which go into complete dormancy during the winter months, pines continue to grow in winter, albeit a lot more slowly. They also start growing in the spring much earlier than their deciduous counterparts.

BELOW: All pines will shed their old needles in the fall. Simply remove them and your pine will look fresh and green.

Feeding

Feeding is best started in early spring with a weak application of a high nitrogen fertilizer. This should be followed in late summer with a dose of low nitrogen fertilizer, such as rapeseed. The Japanese white pine responds to feeding well. If they are not fed regularly, they soon go yellow and lose vigor. Branches and twigs can also die, and new buds will not form readily.

European pines, on the other hand, are not hungry feeders. In fact, overfeeding can do more harm than good, as this causes rapid thickening of the branches, too many terminal buds, and generally coarse growth. Just a weak application of a high nitrogen liquid feed in the early spring is sufficient to keep them in good health.

ABOVE: A pine is trained into the desired shape using wire. Check that the wires are not too tightly wrapped around the branch to avoid unwanted marks.

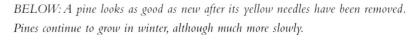

BELOW: A pine looks as good as new after its yellow needles have been removed. Pines continue to grow in winter, although much more slowly.

ABOVE: Fallen needles can be swept up with a rice haulm brush. Tweezers are useful for removing the yellowing needles.

ABOVE: You can also trim back half the new shoots in early summer to keep the foliage pads compact.

ABOVE: Spring is the best time for trimming pines.

Pruning

All pines grow new buds on old wood easily if given the right treatment. The European pines, and the Scots in particular, respond well to pruning. They will produce new buds by June if the candles are removed or cut in the spring. If the tips of the branches are cut back in June, July, or August, new buds on old wood will be produced by September. If you plan your program of pruning carefully, you can create the ideal pad of branches in just a couple of growing seasons.

The Japanese white pine also produces new buds when pruned, but do not prune after August, as North American summers are not long enough to harden off the new shoots that are produced from August to September. If the pads on the branches get too congested, they will need to be thinned out every three or four years.

The flowers on Japanese white pines should be removed as soon as they appear. Leaving them on can weaken a bonsai. They will also leave ugly gaps on the branches when the flowers finish.

Watering

Most conifers require less water than deciduous trees, and this applies to pines. Pine bonsai stand up to drought much better than maples. Consequently, they do not need to be watered as heavily as deciduous trees. In winter, however, make sure that your pines are kept damp, but not saturated. Too much water in winter can rot the roots. The combination of freezing conditions and wet roots is a certain recipe for disaster. On the other hand, don't keep your pines too dry in winter, as the roots can dry out and the tree will die.

Pests and diseases

Keeping your trees healthy and free of disease is essential for creating a good bonsai. It is only with strong trees that you can create beautiful specimens. Pines are susceptible to adelgids, pests that look very similar to white flies. They infest the twigs and branches, and are difficult to get rid of. When they appear on your pines, spray them with an insecticide once every couple of days for about a week. After each application of insecticide, leave the tree for a day or so and then hose off the dead or half-dead insects. A couple of applications of insecticide should soon get rid of the pests completely.

Pines are also prone to root aphis attack. Unfortunately, this can sometimes be confused with the white mycelium that surrounds the rootball of healthy pines. It is only on closer inspection that the aphis can be identified. Treat with a couple of applications of insecticide.

BELOW AND RIGHT: Five needle pines often flower in early spring. This is not a sign of a tree under stress. On the contrary, it is perfectly normal for pines to do this. The flowers should be removed to induce new shoots to develop later in the summer.

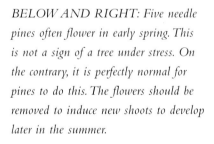

JAPANESE MAPLES

Japanese maples are ideally suited for bonsai. They will grow quite happily in containers and respond well to constant pruning. Their delicate leaf forms and exquisite coloring make them one of the most popular subjects for bonsai work. Japanese maples are extremely hardy. They can withstand temperatures as low as 10°F, although their new leaves in spring can be damaged by late spring frosts. Unfortunately, they will only grow in cool temperate conditions. If you live in an area that has a tropical or even Mediterranean climate, then Japanese maples are not for you.

Suitable species of maple

There are scores of varieties of Japanese maple, most of which are suitable for bonsai. The ordinary mountain maple, *Acer palmatum*, is by far the most commonly used in Japan. In spring, the leaves emerge in various shades of green and bronze, and by autumn, it erupts into brilliant hues of red and gold. The autumn color is quite spectacular and is one of the reasons why this tree is so popular.

Colorful varieties, such as 'Deshojo,' 'Seigen,' and 'Chisio,' are extremely popular for their red leaves in spring, while dwarf varieties, such as 'Kiyohime,' 'Mikawa Yatsubusa,' and 'Shishigashira,' are grown for their dense, bushy habit.

The trident maple, *Acer buergerianum*, though not strictly a Japanese maple, is very popular for developing thick trunk specimens and root-over-rock designs. This is a fast-growing maple and results can be achieved in a relatively short period of time.

LEFT: 'Deshojo' is one of the most colorful and delightful Japanese maples in the spring. Its carmine hues last for about three months and then change to a mottled greenish-pink in the summer.

RIGHT: An ordinary mountain maple transforms to show the most vivid coloring in the fall. This specimen is growing in the root-over-rock style.

General care

Japanese maple bonsai are fairly easy to keep. Provided they are watered daily, sometimes twice daily on very hot days, they should give you many years of enjoyment. Many bonsai maples are known to be well over one hundred years old.

Bonsai maples should be fed with a high nitrogen fertilizer in spring, and with a low nitrogen fertilizer in late summer. Older specimens that have a fine structure of twigs and branches should not be fertilized too much, or they will develop a thicker growth. Some growers will only use a weak fertilizer, such as rapeseed, in order to maintain the tree's delicate structure of twigs and avoid coarse growth.

Repotting should only be done when the tree is pot-bound and no more than once every two or three years. Repotting at the right time is crucial and should be done when the new buds are just about to break, usually in early spring. The ideal potting mix for bonsai maples is a free-draining, loam-based potting soil. Most bonsai nurseries sell Japanese *akadama* soil, which is ideal, but if this is not available then a loam-based potting soil mixed with one third sharp sand and one third medium grade bark makes a good substitute.

ABOVE: Shigitatsu-sawa is a good variety of maple to use for bonsai. This is the green form, but there is also a red version.

ABOVE LEFT: The higasayama maple produces stunning foliage in the spring. Young bonsai maples should be fed with a high nitrogen fertilizer in spring and with a low nitrogen fertilizer in late summer.

Pests and diseases

When their new leaves emerge, maples are very susceptible to aphid attack. You will need to keep a close eye throughout the spring and summer for aphids if you wish to have unblemished foliage. Aphids are easily controlled by insecticide. Insecticides that contain perimicarb or bifenthrin are very effective. In very wet summers, maples may suffer from mildew. Again, any of the garden chemicals for mildew will soon control the problem. A well ventilated environment with plenty of air circulation will also help reduce the risk of mildew.

LEFT: *Japanese maples grow easily from seed. They can be extremely varied and their color in the fall is just as striking. This is a five-year-old seedling.*

LEFT: *Koto-no-Ito, or the Japanese harp string maple, in the fall.*

OPPOSITE: *A seigen maple as a specimen bonsai.*

Pruning

Maples have two bursts of growth: the first is in early spring and the second in early summer. Long shoots should be pruned back to maintain the original triangular bonsai shape.

Leaf cutting does not reduce the size of the leaves to any significant extent, so it is not worth doing for this reason alone. However, if you forget to water your tree on a hot summer's day, and the leaves shrivel and dry out, you can give the tree a new lease of life by cutting off all the dried leaves, leaving just the leaf petiole. A new crop of leaves will emerge in three or four weeks.

RIGHT: Kiyo-hime maple has vivid green leaves in early spring. This variety is always grown in the broom style.

BELOW: Trident maples are particularly suited for root-over-rock style, as they are extremely vigorous trees.

ABOVE: A mountain maple in the height of summer. Maples should be grown in full sun, as this produces a strong, healthy tree.

Winter care

Maples shed their leaves in autumn and then become dormant. As they are fairly hardy trees, they generally do not need winter protection. However, if you live in an area where the winter temperatures are consistently below freezing, then winter protection is advisable. An unheated greenhouse or dry garden shed is usually sufficient to stave off the worst of the winter frosts.

The ordinary *Acer palmatum* and the red 'Deshojo' are completely hardy in temperate winters and do not require any winter protection. The trident maple, however, does need the protection of a cool greenhouse. 'Seigen' and 'Kiyohime' are hardy in winter, but their foliage requires protection as late spring frosts can disfigure the lovely new leaves that are emerging.

RIGHT: Most maples have a beautiful color in the fall. The maple on the left is the rough bark maple, or arakawa, while the one on the right is a mountain maple in root-over-rock style.

Maples suitable for bonsai

Red varieties: 'Deshojo,' 'Benichidore,' 'Seigen,' and 'Chisio'

Dwarf varieties: 'Mikawa Yatsabusa,' 'Kiyohime,' 'Kashima,' 'Kotohime,' and 'Shishigashira'

Other named varieties: 'Japonicum,' 'Katsura,' 'Yukon,' 'Arakawa,' (rough bark maple), 'Chigosan,' 'Benishidare,' 'Sangokaku,' 'Asahi Zuru,' 'Shigitatsusawa,' 'Enkan,' red and green Dissectum, 'Kinkakure,' 'Benikagame,' 'Nomura,' 'Satsuki Beni,' 'Tsuma Beni,' and 'Seiryu'

Trident maples: various forms, including the variegated varieties

ABOVE: Mountain maple in the clump, or kabudachi, style.

ABOVE: A favorite mountain maple of the author.

ABOVE: Early spring foliage of tsuma gaki maple.

ABOVE: Mountain maple, measuring 4 ft. high, in the twin trunk style.

ABOVE: One of the japonicum maples grown as a formal upright tree.

JUNIPERS

Junipers are one of the most popular evergreen subjects for bonsai. It is a genus that includes many species suitable for bonsai. Most of them are hardy and easy to care for, but they have something which most other species do not possess: a dense and gnarled wood suitable for creating stunning driftwood effects. As a bonus, they also have quite attractive foliage.

All these qualities make them the favorite for demonstration material and raw material for bonsai enthusiasts all over the world. Japanese growers have always liked junipers, and good-quality specimens can command very high prices. There is a vast range of junipers, but when referring to bonsai, there are several that are worth mentioning in detail.

Suitable species of junipers

Of the many junipers suitable for bonsai, the *J. chinensis* species probably has the largest number of varieties suitable for bonsai work. The classic is the one that most bonsai enthusiasts refer to as the "Chinese juniper." This, in fact, is a hybrid species whose Latin name is *Juniperus × media*, a cross between *J. chinensis* and *J. sabina*.

The Japanese call it *shimpaku* or *shinpaku*, which simply means "juniper" in English, and is not much help when trying to find out what the correct variety name should be.

Most Japanese exhibition manuals refer to *shimpaku* as 'Sargentii,' but this seems to be a misnomer, as 'Sargentii' is a ground-hugging juniper with coarse foliage that only vaguely resembles *shimpaku*. The variety that comes closest to the correct botanical description of *shimpaku* is *J. × media* 'Globosa Cinerea.' The confusion does not end here, as there are many types of Chinese juniper that are used for bonsai in Japan, not to mention in Taiwan and China.

In Japan, the favorite among most growers is one with very fine foliage called 'Itoigawa.' It is perhaps the most sought after Chinese juniper, because the foliage is both fine and very compact, and the color is a deep green. Then there is 'Kisoo,' which has a much coarser foliage texture, and 'Tohoku,' which comes from the mountains of the Tohoku region of Japan, again with coarse foliage.

The other popular juniper species for bonsai is *Juniperus rigida* or needle juniper. As its name implies, the leaves are literally as sharp as sewing needles, which makes them a less popular variety when it comes to working on them. However, for sheer drama when creating driftwood effects, this must rank as one of the best. Needle

LEFT: An ancient needle juniper, J. Rigida, *in the formal upright style that belongs to the author. The subtle off-center positioning of the trunk gives it aesthetic balance.*

RIGHT: This Chinese juniper is in the informal upright style. Little bits of driftwood called jins *and* sharis, *or weathered dead wood, emphasize the powerful-looking trunk.*

junipers are usually seen in the formal upright and informal upright style with lots of driftwood.

There are three main varieties of *Juniper rigida*. The standard type has very sharp needles between ½ in. and 1 in. long. The second type also has sharp needles, but they are only about ½ in. long. Finally, there is the dwarf, or *yatsabusa,* type that has less-prickly needles, which are ¼–½ in. long.

The *yatsabusa* type tends to have lovely, contorted trunks and that is why they are sometimes used as the stock for grafting 'Itoigawa' juniper onto its wood. The 'Itoigawa' variety's foliage is much more attractive and is therefore more desirable from the commercial point of view. 'Itoigawa' is also grafted onto 'Kaizuka,' which grows much more quickly.

'Kaizuka' develops a thick trunk in a much shorter time and is therefore more commercially viable for the production of large juniper specimens. It is especially suited for creating bonsai with carved, driftwood effects.

Suitable European varieties

Apart from the above Japanese varieties, there are many other junipers in Europe and America that are suitable for making bonsai. Some are indigenous varieties, while others were introduced to the West by seventeenth- and eighteenth-century plant collectors.

The 'Blaauw' juniper, or *J. × media* 'Blaauw,' is one such example. It originally came from Japan about a century ago, via Blaauw & Co., a Dutch nursery. 'Blaauw' has a bluish-gray tinge, but when grown in a pot as a bonsai, the bluish color turns to a lovely green, making it indistinguishable from the *shimpaku* that is commonly used in Japanese nurseries.

The 'San Jose' juniper, or *J. chinensis* 'San Jose,' originally from California, is becoming more and more popular in the West for bonsai because of the dramatic characteristics of its trunk. Gnarled driftwood effects can easily be achieved on relatively young material, as it is quite a fast grower. Most garden centers stock 'San Jose.'

The other nursery juniper used quite a lot by bonsai enthusiasts is *J. squamata* 'Meyeri.' This is normally a tall, straight juniper and makes suitable material for carving and creating driftwood effects.

J. × media 'Pfitzeriana' is another species of juniper suitable for bonsai. It is very similar to the common *J. chinensis*, but has an unfortunate smell. The foliage of this variety is rather floppy, but regular pinching will keep it compact.

There are many ground cover varieties that are very suitable for creating a cascade bonsai. The best ones are *J. horizontalis* 'Procumbens' and *J. communis* 'Hornibrookii.' They make virtually "instant" and very attractive-looking bonsai.

This list is by no means comprehensive. There are dozens of other species and varieties available that are all highly suitable for bonsai work. Unfortunately, ordinary garden centers do not stock them all. The only place to find really large specimen plants is in nurseries that still grow plants in the open ground. Some specialty bonsai nurseries grow material in the open ground for precisely this kind of work.

Junipers growing in the wild

Junipers can still be found growing in the wild in their natural habitats. In the mountainous regions of Japan and along rivers like the Itoigawa, *J. rigida* and *J. chinensis* grow naturally. However, collecting from the wild is now strictly controlled and sometimes forbidden in some places.

In Europe, a common juniper that resembles *J. rigida* grows in mountainous regions, but should not be collected for environmental reasons. *J. globosa*, found in many Mediterranean countries, such as Spain, Portugal, and Cyprus, is very similar to the Chinese juniper because of its scale-like foliage. It can be found growing along limestone cliffs and hills. Again, the ethical thing to do is always to leave them alone and admire them where they are.

There is an area in the western Himalayas where wild creeping junipers grow. It is rumored that the local villagers use these trees for firewood, but then again they must never have heard of bonsai!

ABOVE: A selection of specimen junipers.

145

RIGHT: *This Chinese juniper 'Blaauw' was styled in 1986 from ordinary nursery stock and shown two years later at the Chelsea Flower Show, England. Here it has just been wired.*

LEFT: *The foliage of the needle juniper is very sharp.*

General care

Junipers are very hardy plants. They do not require winter protection in temperate countries. However, if you are at all worried, then an unheated greenhouse would provide adequate protection from frosts and cold winds.

In commercial nurseries, the imported Chinese junipers and *J. rigida* from Japan are protected in poly-tunnels during the winter. Chinese junipers benefit from protection in green shade tunnels, as this gives them a brighter green foliage in the winter. The shade tunnels keep the frost from turning the foliage brown. If junipers are left in the open during winter, they turn a reddish-gray color, very similar to the winter color of the *J. cryptomeria*. The browning is not detrimental, and in the spring, the foliage will soon turn green again.

Sometimes, Chinese junipers will shed a lot of needles in the spring. The green needles turn yellow and drop off. If this happens, examine the roots to check for root rot. If the roots are not in good condition, then the tree should be potted in sphagnum moss or in a fairly open potting soil to aerate the roots. If the roots are fine, feed with a high nitrogen fertilizer and new needles will soon grow.

Regular pinching is absolutely essential if you are to keep your junipers tight and compact. This also helps to create those lovely rounded mounds of foliage sometimes referred to as "clouds." Trimming with scissors does leave brown marks. If you must use scissors, then make sure you cut into the woody shoots and not the green foliage to avoid leaving marks.

A Chinese juniper bonsai that hasn't been pinched for more than thirty years will just become straggly and misshapen, and is no good for anything else but raw material. So don't neglect to pinch the foliage; it is one of the most important chores for keeping junipers looking tight and compact.

Position

In the summer, junipers should be grown in full sun, although the Chinese juniper will have a better color if kept in partial shade, especially when temperatures get too hot.

Do not keep junipers in a position where air circulation is poor, as this can encourage unwanted diseases, such as scale, mildew, and

rust. Inadequate light and poor air circulation will always result in sickly looking trees.

Watering

Junipers require less water in summer than deciduous trees, but they will still need watering daily from March to early October, unless there has been heavy rain. In winter, they should be kept on the dry side, but watering should not be overlooked, especially if your trees are spending the winter in an unheated greenhouse. It is so easy to forget that trees kept under cover will not get any rain, so watering is still necessary to keep them moist. The soil should be damp, but not saturated or completely dry.

Soil

The potting soil needed for junipers is very similar to that used for pines. An open, sandy medium is best. A mixture of one part *akadama* and one part coarse sand, with perhaps a little bit of forest bark, is good. If you prefer using a loam-based potting soil, then equal portions of this mixed with forest bark and sharp sand makes a good potting medium.

Feeding program

All bonsai need regular feeding, and junipers are no exception. If they are not fertilized regularly, they will turn a sickly yellow color, and the tree will become weaker and weaker, and could eventually die. Sparse foliage is usually a sign of a poorly maintained tree.

Start the feeding program in the early spring with an application of a high nitrogen fertilizer. The Japanese 10-10-10 or 8-8-8 fertilizer is good. The fertilizer pellets can be left on the surface of the soil for

LEFT: Driftwood detail on the author's ancient Juniper rigida.

the rest of the year, and in July, rapeseed pellets can be used to harden off the growth for the winter. This is all the feed that is needed. If your trees are not fed regularly, they will not stay healthy, and it will be difficult to maintain their shape and form.

Pests and diseases

Junipers are not prone to many pests and are also relatively free from disease. Aphids seldom host on junipers, but scale is a problem. Unfortunately, not many people can spot scale on their trees, as they are so minute in size—usually smaller than a pinhead. If scale is left untreated, it can cause serious problems. As the little insects suck the sap from the needles, much of the foliage will drop off, and the tree will get progressively weaker. Most insecticides will get rid of scale. Bifenthrin-based insecticide is very effective.

Vine weevils are becoming an increasing problem in Europe. Fortunately, there are now many forms of biological controls, such as nematodes, which are extremely effective.

Rust can also be a problem with Chinese junipers. One of the reasons why the importation of this species is strictly controlled is because of the risk of this disease spreading to pear and apple orchards in the West.

Some junipers, such as 'Blaauw,' sometimes die off for no apparent reason, and the only possible cause is root rot from phytophtera. The culprit is usually potting soil that is too wet.

Repotting

Repotting is best done in mid to late spring. It is best not to remove too many of the roots when you repot, as repotting does set the tree back.

If any of the roots have rotted, simply cut the dead roots back to the live areas, and new roots should develop fairly soon. Vitamin B solution or Japanese root reviving fluid can also help newly potted trees recover quickly.

A poly-tunnel environment is beneficial immediately after repotting, as it reduces transpiration or moisture loss from the foliage. After repotting, 2–3 weeks in a poly-tunnel environment is all that is needed.

Remember to tie newly potted trees into their pots with wire or string to keep them from being blown or knocked over. Do not feed newly potted trees for at least a month. Fertilizer applied immediately after repotting can damage the ends of vulnerable roots that have just been cut.

Training and shaping

Any time of the year is good for wiring and shaping a juniper tree. Wear gloves, as the needles can sometimes produce an allergic reaction. Lime sulphur is best applied in spring and summer on a warm, dry day. Never apply it in wet conditions, as the lime sulphur can leach into the soil and burn the roots.

ABOVE: Driftwood detail on a needle juniper. Lime sulphur should be applied to the driftwood in early spring.

LEFT: All junipers flower in the spring, followed by berries. Don't let too many berries remain on the tree, as the foliage will not develop properly.

FLOWERING TREES

One of the great delights of growing bonsai is experiencing the changes of the seasons at close quarters, seeing the little trees go through the same cycles as their full-grown counterparts in nature.

With deciduous trees, the seasonal changes are quite obvious: the trees put on new growth in the spring, there are deeper shades of green in summer, and glorious autumn tints come out in the fall.

For the evergreens, the changes are more subtle, but still interesting nonetheless. With trees that flower, the blossom and the fruit that usually follow are added bonuses.

Suitable species of flowering trees

Bonsai that flower have a special place in every bonsai grower's collection. There are many flowering trees and shrubs that make excellent subjects for miniaturizing. Of the deciduous trees, the members of the Rosaceae family are all very suitable for making flowering bonsai. They include cotoneasters, *crataegus* (hawthorns, in particular), *prunus* (flowering cherries and apricots), *chaenomeles* (popularly known as 'Japonica'), *cydonia* (Chinese quince), *malus* (crab apples), and *pyrus* (pear).

Other flowering subjects very suitable for bonsai that are grown both commercially and by amateurs include *albizia*, *aesculus* (horse chestnut), *andromeda*, *camellia*, *cercidiphyllum*, *cornus* (in particular, *C. officinalis*), *euonymus* (spindle tree), *forsythia*, *ilex serrata* (the Japanese deciduous holly), *indigofera*, *Jasminum nudiflorum* (jasmine), *laburnum*, *lagerstroemia* (crape myrtle, which is tropical), *lespedeza* (Japanese bush clover), *lonicera* (the Japanese honeysuckle *L. morrowii* is particularly attractive), *M. stellata* (magnolia), *morus* (mulberry), *pieris*, *potentilla*, *punica* (pomegranate), *pyracantha*, rhododendrons (other than the Satsukis), *ribes*, rose, rosemary, *spirea*, *styrax*, *syringa* (lilac), *viburnum*, *vitex*, and *weigela*. (See the following pages for more information about wisteria and satsuki azalea.)

General care

There is no mystery to growing flowering trees for bonsai. They are trained and shaped in the same way as all other bonsai. The only aspect in which they differ is the fertilizing regime.

For flowering bonsai to bloom well, they need to be fertilized with a high phosphorus and high potassium feed in late summer, in order to induce flower buds to form. The fruiting stems produced in late summer also need to be shortened to three or four buds so that the tree does not lose its shape and still carries enough flowering shoots for the following year. Many enthusiasts find that their flowering bonsai tend to bloom well every other year. This is not unusual, as many fully grown trees behave in this way, too. In orchards, a poor flowering season often follows a good one. It is possible that they like to rest between years, so do not be disheartened; let nature take its course.

Watering should be no different from that for other bonsai, although by late summer, reduced watering may encourage the flowering stems to harden. Flowering subjects should be placed in full sun, as sunshine helps to harden the wood.

Japanese growers recommend repotting of flowering trees immediately after flowering. This can prove troublesome, as many of the flowering trees are in full leaf after flowering. It is preferable to repot them in very early spring. This allows the tree to settle down well before flowering starts. Flowering subjects also seem to prefer deep pots. Otherwise, their shoots die back and they weaken.

Wiring, pinching, and shaping are almost the same as for other bonsai. Just be careful not to prune off all the newly formed flowering shoots in the process.

RIGHT: Even an ordinary dessert apple can be grown as a bonsai. Unfortunately, the fruit seldom reduces in size, making it look a little out of proportion.

LEFT: *A crab apple,* Malus halliana, *known as "Hall's crab," is in full bloom by early spring.*

RIGHT: *The pink buds of the crab apple are just as attractive as the blooming flowers.*

OVERLEAF: *(Left) The golden flowers of forsythia are a welcome sight in early spring. The forsythia here are grown in the root-over-rock style. (Right) A* Wisteria sinensis *always makes a stunning show in the spring.*

Pests and diseases

The pests and diseases associated with flowering trees are no different from that of other trees. However, members of the Rosaceae family (i.e. hawthorns, cherries, apricots, and crab apples) are very prone to rust and mildew problems.

If these varieties are sprayed with the appropriate chemicals, they can be controlled and kept healthy without any trouble. If you want to find out which proprietary brand of chemicals to use, your local nursery or garden center should be able to point you in the right direction.

Fruiting and flowering bonsai give great pleasure, and they are no more difficult to grow and maintain than other nonflowering trees.

LEFT: A Siberian crab apple in full bloom grown in the root-over-rock style. The Japanese ibigawa *rock is in the form of a pool.*

RIGHT: The beauty of a flowering bonsai is unsurpassed.

SATSUKI AZALEA

The Satsuki azalea is one of the most colorful flowering trees for bonsai. Not only are the flowers beautiful, but their tiny leaves and evergreen habit make them one of the most versatile plants. They provide the best of both worlds—a lovely flowering tree in the late spring and a beautiful evergreen for the rest of the year.

Unlike most of the other azaleas, Satsuki is a late bloomer. In mild temperate areas, they bloom in late spring or early summer. In Japan, they usually bloom in the first week of June. In fact the name "Satsuki" is derived from the fifth month of the Asian calendar. Most of the major Satsuki exhibitions in Japan are held in the first week of June when they are at their best.

The Satsuki is one of the many hardy Asiatic hybrid azaleas bred in Japan over the last hundred years. The parentage of the Satsuki is mainly *Rhododendron indicum* × *Rhododendron simsii*. In bonsai manuals, they are often referred to as *R. indicum* or *R. simsii*, both of which are probably correct. Like the parent plants, the Satsuki is also evergreen or semievergreen.

RIGHT: 'Kippo-no-hikari' shows off its red, pink, and pink-and-white striped blooms.

BELOW: Multicolored Satsukis are the show stoppers at exhibitions. This one is the ever popular 'Nikko.'

RIGHT: *One of the most popular Satsukis, 'Nikko' has multicolored dark pink, light pink, striped, and white flowers all on the same tree.*

LEFT: *'Hi-no-tsukasa' is one of many single-colored Satsukis that are available.*

Satsukis are well known for their habit of sporting, which makes the plant all the more interesting and explains the many hundreds of different varieties that have been developed in the past century. Some Satsuki varieties can have as many as three colors of flowers on the same plant.

RIGHT: 'Kinsai' is one of the very popular red Satsukis with long stamens.

General care

As they are hardy plants, they are easy to grow in most of the temperate regions throughout Europe and North America, but not in the tropics. The only protection they need in temperate regions is shade cover to protect them from the worst of the frost; they do not need to be kept in heated greenhouses in winter to survive the cold. They prefer shade both in summer and winter, and need to be kept moist. Fortunately, they are relatively trouble free, as far as pests and diseases are concerned.

Soil

Satsukis are best grown in a special Japanese soil called *kanuma*, which is a very light soil. This is mixed with one third sphagnum moss to promote good root growth. They do not like heavy potting soils or potting soils that do not drain freely. Repotting and branch pruning need to be done immediately after flowering.

Repotting and feeding

In Japan, late June or early July is the traditional time for repotting, because the rainy season provides the hot, humid conditions that encourage vigorous growth. Feeding is best done in late summer, using Japanese rapeseed fertilizer or any of the proprietary flowering fertilizers, such as rose fertilizer.

OVERLEAF: Identifying Satsukis correctly can be quite a task, as there are a few thousand varieties. This is most likely 'Yata-no-kagami.'

Postflowering period

With Satsukis, the postflowering period is the busiest time of the growing season. First, there is the deadheading of the flowers to do. Do not leave the flowers on the tree for longer than is necessary. It is important to get the tree to generate new shoots that will produce the flowers for next year. Trim the tree for shape, and if any branches and twigs need wiring, this should also be done at this time of the year. Before the autumn sets in, you should have finished feeding the tree, and all that remains is to wait until the "fifth" month for your Satsukis to bloom and for you to enjoy them at their best.

Suitable varieties of Satsuki

There are hundreds of different varieties of Satsuki. The two most popular and strongest are 'Kaho,' with pink and white flowers, and 'Gyoten,' with light pink and dark pink flowers. Other popular varieties include 'Suisen,' with red-and-white flowers; 'Kozan,' which has white blooms; 'Korin,' with carmine pink flowers; 'Nikko,' with salmon-pink flowers; 'Kinsai,' with red honeysuckle-shaped flowers; 'Wakebisu,' which has two shades of pink flowers; 'Osakazuki,' with carmine flowers; 'Suisen,' with red-and-white, and pink-and-white flowers; 'Shiryu-no-mai' and 'Chinzan,' with deep pink flowers; 'Hikari-no-tsukasa,' with dark pink and light pink flowers; 'Nyohozan,' with two-tone pink flowers; and 'Yama-no-hikari,' with two-tone, salmon-pink flowers.

Exhibiting

The Satsuki attracts a large following, especially in Japan. There are hundreds of Satsuki bonsai clubs. No other species of tree commands the same enthusiastic following.

Needless to say, there are special exhibitions dedicated to Satsukis, and good specimens still command very high prices. For the average amateur bonsai enthusiast, there could not be a finer variety, for it is as handsome in flower, as when it is not. As well as being beautiful, they are also extremely hardy, making it an excellent choice for bonsai enthusiasts.

WISTERIA

One problem that seems to puzzle most people is how to make a wisteria bloom every year. Many remedies and solutions have been suggested, but few produce consistent results. The wisteria bonsai will flower well the first year, but in subsequent seasons, there will be hardly any flowering at all.

No one seems to know the answer, or if they claim to have solved the problem, it only seems to work for them. When others try their recommendations, they do not produce the desired results. Unfortunately, there seems to be a lot of conflicting advice around. For instance, some suggest immersing a wisteria in a bowl of water throughout the summer to rot the feeder roots and encourage flower buds to form. The other recommendation is not to overfeed during July and August, when the flower buds are forming, to keep the vines and tendrils from taking all the nourishment. Another theory is that the roots need to be heavily restricted or pot-bound in order to induce flower bud production. None of these recommendations are guaranteed to work.

Immersing wisteria in water throughout the summer is a dangerous practice, as this will only serve to rot the roots and may eventually kill the plant. Wisteria do need plenty of water during the growing season, but it is better to water frequently than to stand the tree permanently in a tray of water. If you have to stand the plant in a tray to make the watering easier, then only fill the tray with water for an hour or so each day. Ideally, water them several times a day, and keep a close eye on them to see that they do not dry out.

As for restricting the feed during July and August, there is really no need for this. If you withhold the application of fertilizer, this could result in a starved and sickly plant. Wisteria do not need repotting very often, but they should be moved into larger pots at regular intervals. Leaving them to become pot-bound is not the answer either.

Wisterias that are planted as ordinary climbers to creep up a wall or pergola, flower profusely year after year. They grow vigorously, and produce strong tendrils and lots of foliage, yet they still end up with huge bunches of spectacular blossoms each spring. Their roots have not been rotted by standing them in water, nor have the roots been restricted in any way. So where does the answer lie? The key to all this must be the nourishment that the plant receives through the soil.

On my visits to Japan, I have observed how wisteria intended for bonsai are developed. Young grafted plants are grown in the fields to thicken up their trunks. The fields chosen for wisteria are usually ones that have been used for growing rice the previous year. Rice paddy fields are heavily fertilized, using both organic and inorganic fertilizer, and there is a lot of well-rotted organic material in the soil. Consequently, the wisteria that are grown in these fields are strong, vigorous, and heavily loaded with flower buds for the following spring.

Growing wisteria in bonsai pots deprives them of the vital nourishment they need for flower bud formation. There are two ways of overcoming this problem. The first is to feed them heavily immediately after flowering with a spring fertilizer (either 8-8-8 or 10-10-10). This is a high nitrogen feed that promotes strong growth and makes the leaves green. Plants fed with this fertilizer will not suffer from chlorosis or yellowing of the leaves. Leave this fertilizer on for the rest of the year. Later on in midsummer, feed the wisteria with rapeseed fertilizer. Put a large handful of the fertilizer on the surface of each pot and leave it there for the rest of the year.

Strong tendrils will start to grow in summer. Leave the tendrils on the plant for about a month, because the tendrils help to strengthen the tree and also help to develop a good root system. Cut the long tendrils back to three or four buds, which will bear next year's crop of flowers, in late summer or early autumn.

RIGHT: Wisteria floribunda, *or the Japanese wisteria, is very popular as a bonsai. The long racemes of pale purple flowers in the early spring are simply breathtaking.*

When it comes to repotting, this technique does create some confusion, because some Japanese bonsai books advocate repotting after flowering, while others recommend repotting in the early spring. In the West, it is best to repot most bonsai in the early spring, which is much safer than when the plant is in leaf after flowering.

Keeping wisteria in their bonsai pots year in and year out puts the plant under strain. Give the plants a vacation every so often by transferring them into large flower pots planted with either *akadama* or peat-based potting soil. This strengthens the plant and gives them a new lease of life.

Generous feeding, therefore, seems to be the answer, with plenty of rapeseed fertilizer or well-rotted horse manure. Rose fertilizer also helps, but is not a substitute for rapeseed.

Growing wisteria in full sun is also important, as the sunshine helps to ripen the new shoots that carry next year's flower buds. As with most plants, sunshine, food, and water are the essential ingredients for strong, healthy growth, and for wisteria bonsai, the same principles apply with the addition of a heavy application of rapeseed fertilizer.

RIGHT: Wisteria sinensis, or Chinese wisteria, is equally attractive if not superior to Wisteria floribunda as a bonsai because the flowers are very fragrant. This is the blue or mauve form. There are others which are pink and some which are pure white.

Reference

BONSAI WEBSITES

Bonsai, as you might expect for such a well-established and internationally based hobby, has a substantial presence on the net. The sites listed here are not necessarily the best—although most are very good indeed—but do give an idea of what's available.

Herons Bonsai
www.herons.co.uk

The starting point is author Peter Chan's own website for Herons Bonsai, one of the best Bonsai nurseries in Europe.

It boasts:
* Seven acres of Bonsai and Japanese garden trees
* Thousands of Bonsai in every shape, size, and style
* Young starter material and extra-large field-grown trees
* Japanese and British specimens of the highest quality
* Pots, tools, toils, and Japanese garden accessories
* Bonsai classes
* Japanese garden design and construction

The related www.heronsjapanesegardens.co.uk

Shows Peter's donation to Wisley of his Chelsea-winning exhibit.

SHOPPING
There are many fantastic on-line shopping facilities. Two good ones are:

Dallas Bonsai Garden
www.dallasbonsai.com/store/index.html

PLANT SHOP
store.yahoo.com/phylum/bonsaiplants.html

SOCIETIES AND CLUBS
Bonsai Clubs International
www.bonsai-bci.com/index2.html

The starting point for any web-related search for information on bonsai is the Bonsai Clubs International website. This identifies BCI as a nonprofit educational organization that "advances the ancient and living art of bonsai and related arts through the global sharing of knowledge."
It has an excellent Index of Bonsai Species (by both botanical and common names) that "consists of guidelines for the care of tree species as compiled from postings on various lists and newsgroups, from several bonsai periodicals and standard bonsai reference works, and from practical experience."
It also provides excellent links to other bonsai-related sites, collections, and exhibits, as well as websites of related interest.

American Bonsai Society
www.absbonsai.org/new.html

The official American Bonsai Society website gives details on membership, events, educational programs, a book catalog, a quarterly journal, and other published works, as well as beginner and advanced articles to help you grow as an artist, and details of clubs in your area. When you travel, see if there is a meeting in that area.

There are many individual clubs, worldwide and local, such as:

Pittsburgh Bonsai Society
www.ccia.com/~tlryan/pbs_main.htm

The PBS provides a good website with a gallery.

Golden State Bonsai Federation
www.gsbf-bonsai.org

The GSBF is an organization formed from member bonsai clubs in California.

Australian Associated Bonsai Clubs
www.bonsaisite.org/aabc

The AABC has a membership of thirty-two clubs and societies throughout the country.

The Federation of British Bonsai Societies
freespace.virgin.net/kath.hughes/index.html

The FoBBS is the principal coordinating body for bonsai clubs in the U.K.

Latin American Bonsai Federation
www.felab.com

Swedish Bonsai Society
home1.swipnet.se/~w-11388/bon_en.htm

Internet Bonsai Club
www.internetbonsaiclub.org

The Internet Bonsai Club describes itself as "a mailing list and a newsgroup dedicated to the art of bonsai." There is a rider: "Joining is easy, but be aware that a considerable amount of mail is exchanged every day. This means anywhere from 50-150 messages a day." Joining gives access to:

* A diagnosis center
* Book reviews
* Interactive galleries for exchanges and discussions between members
* Story sharing—a page for members to share pictures, stories, etc.
* Member bonsai gallery
* On-line bonsai classes

OTHER SITES OF INTEREST

The Bonsai Guide
www.bonsainl.nl

This Dutch site advertises:
* A large collection of Bonsai photographs
* A comprehensive guide to bonsai in Europe
* Picture reports of bonsai exhibitions and bonsai centers
* Links to bonsai tree care guides, suppliers, clubs, newsgroups, courses, and shows.
* Recommendations for bonsai books for beginners.

Nippon Bonsai Association
www.jinjapan.org/kidsweb/virtual/bonsai/bonsai.html

This interesting children's page is good fun, covering:
* What are bonsai?
* Bonsai care techniques
* Mini bonsai gallery

* Virtual bonsai—enables you to try it yourself
* Bonsai tools

Bonsai Empire
members.home.nl/j.b.jonker/

Care, training, experiences, styles, creation, a quiz, the four seasons, gallery, chat—a good site to visit.

Bonsai Worldwide Webring
www.bonsaiworldwidewebring.com

Links to many interesting sites all over the world.

BonsaiSearch.com

www.bonsaisearch.com

A useful bonsai index and directory that provides an at-a-glance comparison of bonsai retailers, along with useful bonsai reference information. Subjects include pottery, tools, accessories, soil, fertilizer, books, and tables. Also has pictures of bonsai, an online bonsai icon collection, and a link to the USDA Plant Hardiness Zone Map.

Bonsaiweb.com

www.bonsaiweb.com

A site with many featured areas, including an information section, a beginner's guide, discussions, tree critique, tree care, a clubs and events section, a virtual show, and a supplies section containing: classifieds, marketplace, books, tools, seeds, and vendors. Links to sites.

UConn plant database

www.hort.uconn.edu/plants

This is a fantastic resource for bonsai or any other plant and is listed by Latin or common names.

FURTHER READING

Other books by the author:

Chan, Peter: *Bonsai—The Art of Growing and Keeping Miniature Trees*; Quintet Publishing, 1985.

Chan, Peter: *Bonsai Masterclass*; The Paul Press, 1987.

Chan, Peter: *Create Your Own Bonsai From Everyday Garden Plants*; Ward Lock, 1989.

Chan, Peter: *The Complete Book of Bonsai—An Inspirational Guide*; Bracken Books, 1989.

Recommended reading:

Adams, Peter D. and Jordan, Bill (photographer): *Bonsai Landscapes*; Ward Lock, 1999. Gives instructions on how to create thirteen individual landscapes, listing components, methods of assembly, feeding, and watering needs. Provides information on tools and materials, and choosing and shaping plants.

Adams, Peter D. and Jordan, Bill (photographer): *The Art of Flowering Bonsai*. A bonsai expert and a top photographer have created a beautiful book covering flowering bonsai and featuring ten plants in detail—Japanese flowering apricot, satsuki and kurume azaleas, cotoneaster, firethorn (pyracanthra), crab apple, white and red hawthorn, deciduous holly, pomegranate, quince, and wisteria.

Ainsworth, John: *Indoor Bonsai*; Ward Lock, 1991. Forms part of the Practical Gardening series; some color pictures and drawings give a basic introduction.

Aragaki, Hideo and Bester, John (translator): *Classic Bonsai of Japan*; Kodansha, 1989. Expensive, definitive guide with over 200 illustrations.

Busch, Werner M. and Wilson, Andrew (translator): *Indoor Bonsai for Beginners: Selection, Care, Training*; Ward Lock, 1997. Good general information for beginners, including description of styles, basics of propagating, shaping, training, pruning, wiring, caring, position, light, temperature, humidity, airflow, soil, watering, fertilizers, pests and diseases; good A-Z of indoor bonsai species.

Coussins, Craig: *Bonsai for Beginners*; Sterling, 1998. Good general starter book.

Giorgi, Gianfranco and Jahn, Victoria (editor): *Simon and Schuster's Guide to Bonsai*; Simon and Schuster, 1991. A very good reference book. There is a picture and general care for all tree types listed. More then 100 full-color photographs of 150 species of trees.

Gustafson, Herb L.: *Keep Your Bonsai Alive & Well*; Sterling, 1997. Problems of bonsai care and maintenance answered. Illustrated with over 150 color photographs.

Gustafson, Herb L.: *Keep Your Bonsai Perfectly Shaped*; Sterling, 1997. Good illustrations mix practical consideration with aesthetics.

Gustafson, Herb L.: *Making Bonsai Landscapes: The Art of Saikei*; Sterling, 1999. Good, and plentiful, images illustrate the concept of depth in a landscape and the main elements of style (harmony, consistency, balance, scale, and interest).

Gustafson, Herb L.: *The Bonsai Workshop*; Sterling, 1996. Care essentials throughout the seasons by regions. Answers to author's 100 basic questions concerning bonsai. Nearly 500 illustrations, glossary and a reading list.

Koreshoff, Deborah R.: *Bonsai Its Art, Science, History and Philosophy*; Timber Press, 1997. Bonsai form, care, and exhibition, illustrated with line drawings and some color photographs. Practical with good chapters on soil and styling. An excellent book.

Lesniewicz, Paul: *Bonsai in Your Home: An Indoor Grower's Guide*; Sterling, 1997. Standard info on history, care, shaping, and creating forms, creating groupings, propagating plants from seed and cuttings, trimming leaves, and pruning roots. Includes an A-Z listing of forty-two bonsai plants with care instructions.

Lewis, Colin: *Bonsai—A Hamlyn Care Manual*; Hamlyn, 1997. Beautiful photos in a general book that has a good directory on major types of tree and all the usual information on pots, basic cultivation, and training.

Lewis, Colin: *Bonsai Survival Manual: Tree by tree guide to buying, maintaining, and problem solving*; Storey Books, 1996. Comprehensive information and horticultural profiles of fifty popular commercial varieties, with information on their specific requirements and a guide to techniques. Color photographs illustrate the subject starting from seeds and cuttings.

Liang, Amy: *The Living Art of Bonsai: Principles & Techniques of Cultivation & Propagation*; Sterling, 1995. Book for beginners, excellent photos; covers history, basic styles, plant training and propagation methods, and, unusually, traditional Chinese aspects of bonsai.

Naka, John Yoshio: *Bonsai Techniques I*; Bonsai Institute of California, 1984. Naka, John Yoshio: *Bonsai Techniques II*; Bonsai Institute of California, 1998. The definitive books on bonsai—volume I covers techniques and styles; volume II covers roots, trunks, branches, apex, styling, containers, and displaying.

Tomlinson, Harry and Bown, Deni: *101 Essential Tips: Bonsai*; Dorling Kindersley, 1996. Basic guide for beginners, covering tools, wiring, shaping, and tips. Quite a good bonsai A-Z section, with pictures and information on care.

Tomlinson, Harry: *Bonsai-pocket encyclopedia*; RD Home Handbooks, 1995. Good guide for beginners, covering every aspect of bonsai; full-color guide to the identification, growing, and training of over seventy-five bonsai trees and shrubs. Step-by-steps show how to shape your bonsai.

Tomlinson, Harry: *The Complete Book of Bonsai*; Dorling Kindersley, 1990. Excellent general guide for the beginner with many color photographs; step-by-steps on cultivation and maintenance; compendium of shrubs and trees.

Bonsai Magazines

Bonsai Today; Stone Lantern Publishing
Bonsai; Bonsai Clubs International (B.C.I.)
Bonsai; Journal of the American Bonsai Society
Bonsai; Smithfield Publishing Ltd.
Bonsaika; Shizen Communication Sarl (in French)
Golden Statements Magazine; Golden State Bonsai Federation

COLLECTIONS

This is a selection of the sites in which one can see collections of bonsai. Further information can be gathered from such websites as Bonsai in Asia (**www.geocities.com/Tokyo/Palace/7574/**) and from many of the sites identified below.

AUSTRALIA
• Auburn Japanese Gardens, New South Wales.
• Brisbane Botanic Gardens, Brisbane, Queensland.
www.brisbane.qld.gov.au/community_facilities/parks_gardens /gardens/mtcootha_botanic_garden/index.shtml
• Koreshoff Bonsai Nursery, Sydney.
• Imperial Bonsai Nursery and Japanese Garden, Sydney.
www.zip.com.au/~elanora/bonindex.html

BELGIUM
• Belgium Bonsai Museum, Lochristi
club.ib.be/f.jacobs/bcg/bcge.htm

CANADA
• Minter Gardens, British Columbia.
www.minter.org
• Dr. Sun Yat-Sen Classical Chinese Garden, Vancouver, British Columbia.
www.vancouverchinesegarden.com
• Les Bonsai Enr, St-Joachim de Shefford, Québec.
lesbonsais.cyberquebec.com
• Montreal Botanical Garden, Montréal, Québec.
www.ville.montreal.qc.ca/jardin/en/japonais/bonsais.htm

CHINA
• Beijing Botanical Garden, Beijing
• Shanghai Botanic Garden, Shanghai.
www.sinosource.com/SH/PUB/SHBG
• Suzhou Gardens, Suzhou, Jiangsu.
www.szgarden.com.cn

GERMANY
• Bonsai-Centrum and Museum of Paul Lesniewicz, Heidelberg.
www.bonsai-centrum.de

INDONESIA
• Bonsai Indonesia, Jakarta.
www.bonsai-indonesia.com/english/index.htm

ITALY
• Crespi Bonsai & Museum, Milan.
www.crespibonsai.it

JAPAN
• Takagi Bonsai Museum of Art, Tokyo

KOREA
• Punjae Artpia (Bonsai Art Park), Cheju-do

SINGAPORE
• The Chinese and Japanese Garden, Singapore

SPAIN
• El Museo Municipal de Bonsái de Alcobendas.
www.davidbenavente.com/museo.htm
• Museo del Bonsai, Marbella.
www.sopde.es/cultura/museos/museo20.html

U.K.
• Birmingham Botanical Gardens and Glasshouses, Birmingham (The National Bonsai Collection)
freespace.virgin.net/kath.hughes/page11.html
• Wisley Gardens. See:
www.heronsjapanesegardens.co.uk/example0.htm
for information on Peter Chan's bonsai at Wisley.

U.S.
• Birmingham Botanical Gardens, Birmingham, Alabama.
www.bbgardens.org
• Northern California Bonsai Collection, Oakland, California.
www.gsbf-bonsai.org/collection.htm
• Southern California Bonsai Collection, San Marino, California.
www.huntington.org
• San Diego Wild Animal Park, Escondido, California.
www.sandiegozoo.org/wap
• The National Bonsai and Penjing Museum (U.S. National Arboretum), Washington D.C.
www.bonsai-nbf.org
• Morikami Museum and Japanese Garden, Delray Beach, Florida.
www.morikami.org
• Fuku-Bonsai Cultural Center & Hawaii State Bonsai Repository, Kurtistown, Hawaii.
www.fukubonsai.com
• Chicago Botanical Gardens, Glencoe, Illinois.
www.chicagobotanic.org
• Des Moines Botanical Center, Des Moines, Iowa
• The Larz Anderson Bonsai Collection of the Arnold Arboretum of Harvard University, Jamaica Plain, Massachusetts.
www.arboretum.harvard.edu/
• Como Park Conservatory, Saint Paul, Minnesota.
www.stpaul.gov/depts/parks/conserv.htm
• Brooklyn Botanical Garden, Brooklyn, New York City.
www.bbg.org
• The International Bonsai Arboretum, Rochester, New York.
www.internationalbonsai.com
• North Carolina Arboretum, Asheville, North Carolina.
www.ncarboretum.org
• Franklin Park Conservatory and Botanical Garden, Columbus, Ohio.
www.fpconservatory.org
• Krohn Conservatory, Cincinnati, Ohio.
www.cinci-parks.org
• Longwood Gardens, Kennett Square, Pennsylvania.
www.longwoodgardens.org
• Phipps Conservatory, Pittsburgh, Pennsylvania.
www.phipps.conservatory.org/index1.html
• Central Texas Bonsai Exhibit, Wimberley, Texas.
www.wimberley-tx.com/~bonsaijg/tree.html
• Elandan Gardens, Ltd, Bremerton, Washington.
www.kitsap.net/tour/portorchard/elandan.html
• Pacific Rim Bonsai Collection, Weyerhaeuser Corporate Campus, Washington.
www.weyerhaeuser.com/aboutus/whereweoperate/ worldheadquarters/bonsaicollection.asp